T0013658

PRAISE FOR

Healing Wisdom
for Pet Loss

"As someone who deals with grief and loss of pets on a daily basis, I am eager to share this book with clients as an invaluable resource for helping them through the hardest part of pet ownership. Anne Marie provides wonderful insight to the dynamic challenges of pet loss and the grief that accompanies it in an inclusive and accepting way. Her exercises and writing prompts are so helpful for learning to cope before, during, and after the loss of a beloved pet."

— DR. ISABEL WYLIE, VMD

"Losing a pet is among the most painful and transformational experiences that a person can have. . . . *Healing Wisdom For Pet Loss* is an important and eloquently written book that presents valuable knowledge for pet owners and their mental health providers. I will keep one in my clinical office to loan to clients who have recently lost a pet and at my academic office for students to borrow."

— ROBERT H. RICE, JR., PHD, LMHC,
Professor, Mental Health Counseling Program Chair,
St. John Fisher University

"I understand the unique bond that we have with our beloved pets and the devastation felt when they are lost. This book provides useful tools to help people, including expressing one's feelings in writing, and ways to honor our cherished family members. I appreciate it also addresses hospice and end-of-life decisions. I keep a copy in my hospital."

— KAREN RAVANESI, DVM

"Written with sensitivity and understanding, *Healing Wisdom for Pet Loss* offers a unique look at our grief reactions related to our pets. . . . I particularly liked this volume's focus on the diverse reactions that people experience, and how working through grief is an individual process that might be different from the reactions of others. I am pleased to recommend this book for all who live with companion animals as well as those who work alongside them. It is a thoughtful and very useful addition to the literature."

—RISË VANFLEET, PHD, RPT-S, CDBC, CAEBC-I, founder and president of International Institute for Animal Assisted Play Therapy® and coauthor of *Animal Assisted Play Therapy*

"*Healing Wisdom for Pet Loss* is an essential guide for anybody who has loved and lost their faithful, cherished pet. Her compassionate support affirms the ache in a grieving heart and provides tools and resources needed to navigate the grief path. This is a comforting and practical must-read!"

—LENA KIELISZAK, LMHC NCC, Rochester, NY

"Grief leaves a hole in our hearts that surfaces and never quite goes away completely. Finding ways to diminish the sharp cut of loss is so necessary to continue on. *Healing Wisdom for Pet Loss* is a labor of love and hopefully will ease the painful loss of a pet for every reader."

—CATHERINE ROMAINE BROWN, author of *The Jack Russell Terrier: Courageous Companion* and *The Jack Russell Terrier: An Owner's Guide to a Happy, Healthy Pet*

"*Healing Wisdom for Pet Loss* is a gift of love for anyone who is experiencing the loss of a cherished pet. Farage-Smith provides the reader with a deeper understanding of the experience of losing their pet and the tools and techniques to help them move through their grief. The author brings her experience as a mental health counselor and her own journey of loving and losing pets to the reader."

—NANCY E. HARRIS, LMHC

"Remembering and honoring our pets when they pass on is essential to our own adjustment and healing from this loss. Farage-Smith presents a wide variety of creative and thoughtful ways to remember and memorialize our beloved pets. As someone who has experienced pet loss, I highly recommend this compassionate and knowledgeable author on this very important book on a loss that needs to be recognized and validated."

—PATRICIA M. CASEY BSW

"Farage-Smith has created a much-needed, thorough, and practical guide for pet loss. Amidst shared companionship with our beloved pets, we inevitably face the decisions and experiences of our cherished animals dying. Farage-Smith draws on her rich experience as a licensed mental health counselor to offer clear, thoughtful, and compassionate guidance to help in these difficult situations. What an insightful handbook for every pet companion/owner."

—PATRICIA EAGLE, author of *Being Mean: A Memoir of Sexual Abuse and Survival* and *Dog Love Stories: How My Dogs Taught Me to Be a Better Human*

"Our pets are family, and grieving for them as we do for humans is natural. *Healing Wisdom for Pet Loss* is an indispensable guide to dealing with the inevitable loss of our beloved companions."

—JONATHAN LOSOS, director, Living Earth Collaborative, Washington University, and author of *The Cat's Meow: How Cats Evolved from the Savanna to Your Sofa*

"*Healing Wisdom for Pet Loss* is an impactful and informative book that reaches out to the source of our grieving. The exercises and suggestions help each reader to manage and work through grief, allowing a new, hopeful perspective to emerge."

—LIZ VALLES, DVM

Healing Wisdom
for Pet Loss

Healing Wisdom
for Pet Loss

An Animal Lover's
Guide to Grief

Anne Marie Farage-Smith, LMHC

SHE WRITES PRESS

Published 2024
Printed in the United States of America
Print ISBN: 978-1-64742-676-7
E-ISBN: 978-1-64742-677-4
Library of Congress Control Number: 2023921068

For information, address:
She Writes Press
1569 Solano Ave #546
Berkeley, CA 94707

Interior design by Stacey Aaronson

She Writes Press is a division of SparkPoint Studio, LLC.

Names and identifying characteristics have been changed to protect the privacy of certain individuals.

This book is dedicated to my mom, Mary, in gratitude for her unconditional love and unfailing wit, wisdom, and inner strength. Her support gave me the courage to keep going, no matter how rocky the road. Her guiding spirit lives on in me and inspired me to pursue this dream of authoring this very special book.

Contents

SECTION III
Coping with Grief

SECTION IV
Moving Forward

How to Use This Book

This book was written for you, whether your cherished pet has already died or you anticipate your pet passing due to a terminal illness, advancing age, or some other situation. This is a guidebook for you to work through and be supported in your grief. Feel free to read it from cover to cover initially or to read select chapters that relate to your own specific situation.

For example, if your need to feel better outweighs your need to systematically learn about this topic, you may want to go to Chapter 9 (Taking Care of You) first.

Additionally, if any of the following are true, you may want to read Chapter 6 (Understanding Types of Grief, Part 1: Anticipatory Grief) first or second. Then, read the part of Chapter 7 on ambiguous grief.

- 🐾 You have just received a diagnosis of a fatal disease or medical condition in your pet.
- 🐾 You have noticed a decline in your pet due to advancing age.
- 🐾 You may have to find a new home for your pet, either temporarily or permanently.
- 🐾 You are considering hospice care or euthanasia for your pet.

If your pet has died or is otherwise gone, Chapter 6 may not be useful for you at this time.

My goal for this book is to provide information you may need now or in the future. Please think of this book as your guidebook in helping you on your own very personal grief journey.

Foreword

Muffin was a rescue dog, a mix of Chihuahua and who-knows-what-else, an adorable and shy twelve pounds of love. She had survived some apparently rough early years by chasing and eating geckos and fallen mangoes in Central Florida. Unfortunately, she had also contracted heartworm disease. The Naples Humane Society found and treated her, and shortly after we adopted her, she was declared cured.

Muffin acted so crazy sometimes that we nicknamed her "Nut." When I did my exercises on the yoga mat, she would incessantly lick the soles of my feet. When the cats tried to get close to her, she would growl and give me the side-eye, knowing I wouldn't punish her. The veterinarian, when we told him that Muffin was age three when she was rescued, laughed and said, "Yes, that's like a used car that they tell you has twelve thousand miles on it. They turned back the odometer on this one." Muffin was probably six or so.

It was impossible not to love her and her antics. She approached each day with boundless enthusiasm. We enjoyed years of joyful companionship. Her belief in me was truly beyond anything I could actually be or do as a human. Sadly, it turned out that the heartworm disease had damaged her heart muscle. She began collapsing upon exertion, or when she was excited (squirrel!). She was prescribed medicine, and then more medicine, and eventually lots of medicine. Her little body swelled with fluid, the last stages of heart disease. And then, long before I was ready, it was her time.

Carl Jung, the famous psychiatrist, talked about *synchronicity*—the idea that sometimes apparently random occurrences are not random at all, but meaningful coincidences that have a direct and significant relation to our lives and experience. Shortly after Muffin passed, Anne Marie Farage-Smith contacted me and asked if I would write a foreword to her new book about pet loss and grief. Wow! What a timely incidence of synchronicity.

I was first introduced to Anne Marie when I was a faculty member and director of the master's degree program in mental health counseling at St. John Fisher University in Rochester, New York, and she had just entered as a graduate student. Immediately upon getting to know Anne Marie, she impressed me with her big heart, her gentle spirit, and her dedicated interest in the animal–human bond. I had been certified as a companion-animal therapist through Cornell University, so we certainly had much in common, and as a psychotherapist myself, I had worked with many clients suffering the throes of grief over the loss of a companion animal. I was delighted to learn that Anne Marie had further developed that interest and had decided to write this important book.

Anne Marie's book that you hold in your hands is helpful for therapists and laypersons alike; it explains the background and research on grief and loss in general, the human–animal bond, and the different ways in which we both anticipate and experience loss of a companion animal. Perhaps most importantly, it provides practical steps for moving through the grieving process, along with specific recommendations for activities to help us through those difficult times.

Anne Marie's empathy and caring radiate from every page of this book, from her very personal perspective as a pet parent, as well as her point of view as a trained and experienced mental health counselor. Her dedication to this vital work is demonstrated not only through her daily work as a therapist, helping people affected by the loss of a beloved pet, but also through her founding of a center to educate and inform the community about this work.

Reading through the pages of *Healing Wisdom for Pet Loss—An Animal Lover's Guide to Grief* helped me, as well, to reflect upon my own grieving process. I am able to mourn the loss of Muffin, to treasure her indomitable spirit and our years together, and to keep her in my heart for as long as memory lives on.

—SIGNE M. KASTBERG, PHD, LMHC,
author of *Servants in the House of the Masters: A Social Class Primer for Educators, Helping Professionals, and Others Who Want to Change the World* (2007) and *Feeling the Call: Therapeutic Uses of Traditional West-African Drumming* (2018)
August 2020

Introduction

*"If there ever comes a day when we can't be together,
keep me in your heart. I'll stay there forever."*

—A. A. MILNE, WINNIE THE POOH BOOK SERIES

 f you have lost a beloved pet or anticipate losing one soon, I wrote this book for you. We will begin to work through the anguish of your grief and get to a hopeful place. I hope this book brings you understanding and comfort. Your grief journey is unique and personal to you. As you turn each page of this book, know that I have also grieved this loss many times. I understand the deep feelings of anguish that can occur when we lose a cherished pet. Without a doubt, they are our very special companions and family members. They enter our lives and provide us with immeasurable love. The day they become one with us in our family is one of the happiest days. The day they die is one of the most heartbreakingly difficult times of our lives. It is my greatest wish for you that this book speaks to you in a special way and helps you to understand and cope with this unique loss.

My own dog Wishbone is but just one example of what I have personally experienced. Wishbone was both a truly remarkable dog and a very important part of our family. He was a smart, loyal, and handsome Jack Russell terrier with a tricolor coat that was smooth and silky. He was always amusing us with his antics, and defending his yard from the pesky squirrels, making them quickly scamper to safety up a tree. He had a particular marking that was extra special to everyone who loved him. On the back of his head, in his neck area, was a V shape of white fur over his brown-and-black head, like his father, who had the same V-shaped pattern. My mom would lovingly pet Wishbone and gently trace the outline of his V with her fingers, as if to be sure the white fur remained separate from the brown.

I still remember that sad and painful snowy February day and the days that followed. His impending death was anticipated, but still heartbreaking. Our precious Wishbone had been diagnosed with canine cognitive dysfunction, which was manifesting in changes in his behavior. He began to frequently wander into a corner of the room, stay and look at the wall for a while, and then turn and walk back out. He no longer responded to us as he once had, by running to greet us as we returned home. However, he was still willing to receive our love by lying in our arms and cuddling. The good news from the veterinary staff and our own observations was that he did not appear to be in pain or distress. He continued to have an appetite until the day of his passing and was still able to receive our love.

When that day came, I knew in my sad and heavy heart that it was the day he would leave a huge empty space in our lives. He lay in his bed in our family room, and I knew the heart-wrenching reality that was going to unfold. I was in the kitchen cutting vegetables for a hearty minestrone soup, while my husband, Elmer, spent some time with him. In the face of something over which I had no control, I imposed minimal structure on the day: I finished the soup, set it to simmer, and then went into the family room and cuddled with Wishbone. We settled into my favorite recliner together, a chair in which we had spent many hours relaxing and cuddling.

He had lost some of his athletic muscle tone in the past few months, but somehow he felt heavier in my arms. His fur was still silky smooth, and he still responded to my touch at the back of his ears. I relished what were to be my last precious moments with him and began to reminisce about the good times. Memories flooded back of my son, Steven, then a nine-year-old, and the immediate connection he had made with Wishbone when he picked the puppy up from his cozy bed with his siblings. The choice was between two puppies. No words were spoken; Wishbone became one with Steven's arms, and we were ready to bring him home to be a part of our family.

As I cuddled with Wishbone in my favorite chair, I told him I loved him (as I often did) and how very glad I was that he had been a part of our family for sixteen years. A wave of peace came over me as I gazed at my forever pup. Wishbone died peacefully in my arms. I continued to hold him and savor my final moments with him. How grateful I am for that opportunity, and for the opportunity for our son, Steven, to quickly come home and be able to say his final goodbyes to Wishbone.

We were at peace with our decision to allow him to leave when he was ready. I can say this without any doubt: it is never easy to lose a cherished pet. We have such wonderful memories of our beloved Wishbone—smart, loyal, loveable, and a great traveler as he accompanied us on many family road trips.

It was tough to go through this loss. My world turned upside down and I just felt numb . . . did this really happen? I knew the tears would flow, and it was not good to suppress them as they continued to flow. Even though his death was expected, that did not make it any easier. His bed in the family room was now empty. As the reality of his absence permeated the house, I tried to eventually focus and feel some feelings of peace and gratitude knowing that Wishbone shared our lives for sixteen years and brought us much joy. The warmth of his furry body is missing from my life. I can visualize him running around the backyard in anticipation of a possible encounter with a squirrel. Embedded in his DNA, his hunting skills were evident even as he frequently "caught" an unwashed sock in the laundry basket.

As the days unfolded and reality set in, my mind knew Wishbone was no longer with us, but my heart kept trying to push it away. I tried to regain some of the structure in my life that was enhanced by having a pet as part of my family. Sometimes it felt like the very fabric of my being was unraveling. It was a definite adjustment to have him missing from our daily lives, and experiencing that would bring on many emotions and tears as time moved on. For me, it was important to engage in creative outlets to remember Wishbone. As a family, we had a small gathering around the tree he used to run around and chase squirrels and placed a memorial rock there. Going through his photos and creating a PowerPoint presentation really helped us to be grateful for his life and work through his death by focusing on happy memories.

We lose our pets through their death, or because they no longer have the ability to share in our lives. Either experience leaves a large void. They were a part of our family, they were unique, and we had a close loving bond with them. It is no wonder that it hurts so much when they die.

My heart aches when pet grief encounters responses like "It was only a dog/cat," "You can get another one," or "You should be over this by now." The pet that died *cannot* be replaced. It was special, one of a kind, with its own personality and cuteness. There was a *special bond of love*, a mutual bond. Our society needs to recognize and honor this type of loss, because it can be so devastating and it affects so many people. When our loss is minimized and not valued by those around us, it becomes very problematic for us. Where is the support for this loss? When a loss is not validated, we may continually push down our feelings and not fully express them. When feelings are unexpressed and simmer within us, they can set us up for prolonged sadness and for physical symptoms, such as body aches, excessive fatigue, loss of appetite, and sleep disorders.

With this book, I hope to educate and shed some light on the very important topic of pet grief and provide you, the reader, with compassionate guidance and support for dealing with your loss. I also provide information for others who are interested in learning about this devastating loss so they may offer some comfort to others.

My research has taken me to hard statistics, but my heart always knew the extent of the importance of our pets. Perhaps these statistics can be part of the wake-up call. According to the *2017–2018 US Pet Ownership & Demographics Sourcebook*, 38 percent of US households has at least one dog, and approximately 25 percent has at least one cat (American Veterinary Medical Association 2018). Simply put, pets are very important to us. They make our lives richer in meaning.

My wish in these pages is to provide validation for this heartfelt loss and to offer support, understanding, and helpful suggestions to honor the memory of your cherished pet. It is for *you* if you are grieving the loss of a pet. With this book, I hope to help you understand, grieve, and ultimately cope with this loss. I acknowledge your loss!

I thank you for wanting to find out about this unique loss and the grief that arises from it. I know it's not easy to look at this loss head-on and confront it. However, it cannot be put on the shelf—it needs to be addressed. I commend you for picking up this book, reading it, absorbing the messages, and working through your grief. Always remember, you are not alone. Your sadness is real and this loss hurts. I hope this book will help you understand the bond you have with your pet, why this loss is uniquely painful, and the grief you are experiencing.

Both as a licensed mental health counselor in private practice and as an educator, my work with individuals and groups who have experienced this loss has provided me with many opportunities to share in their stories of grief and loss. My work with them, their stories, and my own personal experience of losing several pets, as well as my first encounter with a pet that was gone from my life without warning, have helped me understand the magnitude of the grief that comes from the loss of a pet.

In 2019, I established the Rochester Center for Pet Grief and Loss (https://www.petlossroc.com/). Its mission is to provide counseling and group support to people impacted by the loss of a cherished pet. I also created it to teach the public that pet grief and loss impacts many people (as evidenced by the statistics cited earlier in this introduction) and that this loss needs to be recognized and addressed. The impact our pets have on our lives is enormous.

I have a passion for my work and for the message I share in this book. My mission is to be there for others who are experiencing the loss of a cherished pet. Validating and honoring the loss of a pet is of utmost importance to me, as is amplifying the message that the loss of a pet cannot be pushed aside or marginalized. Instead, this grief needs to be recognized and understood. I don't want this loss and the associated grief to continue to be devalued by our society; the need to grieve the loss of a pet is indeed valid and as deserving of recognition as the loss of a human family member.

Make no apologies or comparisons for your grief. Everyone's grief is their own, and it has no particular timeline. The loss of your pet has changed your life. You will never truly get over this grief, but you will rebuild your life around this loss. I have worked with many people who have reported the benefits and importance of recognizing their grief and working through it.

To support you in this process, I have provided reflective writing experiences at the end of each chapter. They are deliberately open-ended and suitable for all ages (with parental assistance when appropriate). These exercises have proven to be very helpful to my clients in exploring, understanding, and healing from their grief. They can help you express emotions that you haven't allowed yourself to express without filters or judgment. Let whatever thoughts come into your mind flow out into the pen and onto the paper.

Writing can be a very healing experience, so allow yourself to reread these thoughts at a later time and learn how you are moving along. These writing experiences work best after reading and reflecting on the chapter associated with them. However, if you prefer, just do them in the order that is most helpful to you. They are offered as suggestions. You are the best one to decide which ones would be the most helpful for you to complete and when.

I recommend you purchase an attractive, decorative notebook for these writing experiences. Alternatively, you can purchase a plain one and personalize it with stickers and special-colored pens or markers. This will become a memory book about your relationship with your cherished pet. With a notebook, you can preserve your special thoughts and refer to them at another time. Many of my clients grieving over the loss of their beloved pet have completed these writing experiences. They found them helpful and felt a sense of relief to express themselves in this way. They also found them to be healing. I wish this for you as well. Give some of them a try. Before you engage in these experiences, prepare yourself by doing the following:

- 🐾 Going to a quiet place, at a quiet time
- 🐾 Playing some quiet soothing music
- 🐾 Quieting your mind and body (Light stretching or controlled breathing can help)
- 🐾 Being open to the experience

On your journey through this book, you will find the following sections and chapters.

SECTION I:
UNDERSTANDING THE BOND AND WHY IT IS IMPORTANT

The human–animal bond is very real, and whenever something breaks that bond, we have so much to lose. Our pets are members of our families. The chapters in this section provide history on this bond, an understanding of why the loss of our pet family hurts so much, and a celebration of how animals have played a powerful role in the lives of so many people. In order to understand the loss, you first need to understand what has been lost.

Chapter 1: The Human-Animal Bond: The human–animal bond runs very deep, and the nature of the relationship between people and their pets is quite complex. Our pets fill many roles and have many positive impacts upon our lives. When a pet dies or is otherwise lost, the loss can be quite profound.

Chapter 2: Pets, Humans, and Their Health Together: There are many documented ways that our pets benefit our health. These benefits go far beyond exercise.

Chapter 3: Healing Companionship of Pets: Our animals help us in many ways, both as service animals and companions. They can literally save our lives. These accounts of how animals have helped and healed may help you assess and remember how your pet has healed and helped you.

SECTION II:
UNDERSTANDING GRIEF AND LOSS

Key to coping with your grief is the knowledge and understanding presented in these four chapters.

Chapter 4: Adjusting to Your Loss: This chapter contains the ways you can lose your pet and how to adapt to this loss.

Chapter 5: Understanding Your Loss and Feelings: This chapter explains why this loss hurts so much and the feelings it generates.

Chapter 6: Understanding Types of Grief, Part 1: Anticipatory Grief: This grief is for a loss that you anticipate happening in the very near future. It can be due to older age of your pet, a terminal health condition, or possibilities that do not involve the death of your pet. This chapter includes a discussion of some considerations unique to a pending loss by death, including pet hospice and euthanasia.

Chapter 7: Understanding Types of Grief, Part 2: Acute, Ambiguous, Disenfranchised, and Complicated Grief: There are several types of grief that can be encountered, either separately or together. This chapter explains what is unique about each type, so that you can gain knowledge to help you understand and process them.

Chapter 8: Using Tools to Organize Your Thoughts and Feelings: You may be familiar with the work of Elisabeth Kübler-Ross or J. William Worden. Their models or frameworks can help you to understand and process your grief.

SECTION III:
COPING WITH GRIEF

The chapters in this section offer specific recommendations for how to take care of you and the people around you. They are a resource of strategies you can use now and in the future to cope with the flood of emotions you may be experiencing. They are also useful skills to cope with stress and anxiety throughout your life.

Chapter 9: Taking Care of You: This chapter contains helpful ways to take care of yourself right now, as well as ways you can revisit and use later.

Chapter 10: Helping Others Who Are Grieving with You: You may not be the only person grieving from this loss. The information in this chapter can help you to help others who are grieving along with you.

Chapter 11: Remembering and Honoring Your Pet: There are many ways you can honor the memory of your pet. Choose a few things in this chapter to memorialize your cherished pet for now, and then review these suggestions for later use.

SECTION IV:
MOVING FORWARD

Chapter 12: Embracing Change, Recognizing Hope: This chapter wraps things up and encourages you to engage in new opportunities as you continue to adjust to this loss in your life.

I received an unexpected and moving letter in January 2020 from a fourth-grade student that validated the motivation for this work. She was working on a school assignment that involved researching a cause, and she was interested in helping families who have lost a pet. When she was in kindergarten, she was "very sad" when she lost her pet. She asked about the Rochester Center for Pet Grief and Loss and requested some information from me on how I help families experiencing pet loss.

I was deeply moved by this student's request and responded

to it. This young person knew firsthand the importance of reaching out for assistance with this loss. Unfortunately, because of COVID-19 and the resulting closing of schools, the final presentation to her classmates, teachers, and families did not happen. I was saddened by the missed opportunity to personally meet this student, but I was also grateful for her desire to help families through this loss. Her letter inspired me; it encourages me to continue to reach out to society, share how important it is to recognize this type of loss, and not allow it to be devalued.

My wish for you through the pages of this book is for you to explore and understand the emotions and feelings you may be experiencing due to the loss of your cherished pet, and to know that others care and can help. It will allow you to know—really know—that your loss is important and valued. Remember, this is a unique loss, like no other. It deserves a book specially devoted to this loss and the subsequent reactions to it. Come, follow me through this book, and feel confident in moving through your grief, knowing that others care and that I care. You are on your grief journey with me.

I wish you well and much peace.

"Animals don't lie. Animals don't criticize.
If animals have moody days,
they handle them better than humans do."

—BETTY WHITE

SECTION I

Understanding the Bond and Why It Is Important

The bond we have with our pets is strong and powerful, and its benefits are mutual. We as pet parents are enriched in so many ways by their presence in our lives, and they are the recipients of all we do for and with them. To understand our grief and the impact it has on our lives, it is helpful to gain insight into this bond of love we have with our cherished pet. That insight will help us to appreciate why it hurts so much when they leave our lives.

Chapter 1

The Human-Animal Bond

everal of my clients have shared that their relationships with their cherished pets have been more gratifying than some of their relationships with other humans. This may be because they provide us with a pure, unconditional love and nonjudgmental positive feedback. Consider the old proverb: "May I become the kind of person that my dog thinks I already am."

What fuels the unique bond that we can experience with our pets? Is it the unconditional love, loyalty, and nonjudgmental presence in our lives with them? Pets share in our daily lives and routines and share full family memberships.

This chapter addresses the nature of the human–animal bond. What constitutes a pet is much more complex than a simple dictionary definition. The human–animal bond runs very deep, and the nature of the relationship between people and their pets is quite complex. Pets fill many roles and have many positive impacts upon one's life. This bond is mutually beneficial. As a result of this special bond, our pets become our healing helpers and loyal companions. They provide social benefits as well as improving our physical health, emotional health, and general well-being. Everyone enjoys the special loyalties of dogs. Children enjoy some particular benefits stemming from their special relationships with animals.

My wish is for everyone to realize just how strong the bond can be between people and their pets. Maybe then, the grief we experience will be more widely accepted and honored, and we can integrate the death into our lives more effectively. Maybe then, pet loss will no longer be a disenfranchised loss, but a loss that is understood and valued.

THE ORIGINS OF THE HUMAN– ANIMAL BOND

The human–animal bond is a very powerful connection, one that really hurts when it is broken, and it will be helpful to understand why we grieve so deeply when that bond is severed. It has thousands of years of history, and knowing this history is not only interesting but important to understanding the depth and breadth of the bond.

The human–animal bond began over twelve thousand years ago, as a working relationship with various animals (Lagoni, Butler, and Hetts 1994). Animals have been at our sides, offering protection and service to us, whether we were hunting, farming, or performing other acts necessary for everyday life.

Dogs have adapted to living with humans over the past ten thousand years (Hare et al. 2010). They have evolved and been bred specifically to be our companions and friends. Anthropologist Brian Hare has developed a "domestication hypothesis" to explain how dogs morphed from their gray wolf ancestors into the socially skilled animals that we now interact with in many of the same ways we interact with other people. This hypothesis essentially states that wolves already had many hunting and social behaviors that were similar to human behaviors. As wolves learned how to interact with people to share in the proceeds of a hunt, they self-domesticated to improve their interactions, and these changes gave them significant survival advantages.

Our special relationship with dogs is no accident, as they are essentially wolves that have benefited from self-domestication.

Dogs have also been selectively bred through generations to socialize with people. In recent research, MRI scans show that most dog brains respond just as pleasurably to praise from their humans as they do to food, when receiving a reward for correctly completing a task (Carroll 2016). For some dogs, the scans show that praise from their humans is an even more effective incentive than food. The research verified the results of the MRI scans by performing behavioral studies with the same dogs. These behavioral studies showed that the dogs with stronger brain responses from their humans preferentially chose their humans over food for their reward after solving a maze. Dogs who showed equal responses to human praise and food would alternate between choosing their humans and food as their reward. Dogs recognize individual people and can learn to interpret human emotional states from facial expression alone.

The human–animal bond can be formed with any animal with which you have an emotional connection, not just dogs and cats. Although the human–animal bond has certainly existed for millennia, the term "human–animal bond" was officially added to our vocabulary in 1979 (Fine 2015). However, professional work using it dates to the 1960s by Austrian zoologist and ethologist Konrad Lorenz, MD, PhD. He became known at the time for his principle of attachment or imprinting, by which a bond is formed between a newborn animal and its caregiver. The attachment relationship between a dog owner and their dog is functionally similar to that between parent and child (Beck 2014).

The human–animal bond is mutually beneficial. Our pets genuinely enrich our lives, and the close bond we develop with them proves this. The American Veterinary Medical Association's Committee on the Human–Animal Bond defines the human–animal bond as "a mutually beneficial and dynamic relationship between people and other animals, that is influenced by behaviors that are essential to the health and well-being of both. This includes, but is not limited to, emotional, psychological, and physical interactions of people, other animals, and the environment" (JAVMA 1998). We clean and fill the pet food bowls daily. Cozy beds are in place, and physical exams take place. All these are definitely necessary in caring for our pet, but the all-important mutual love we receive and give to our pets is without a price tag. Our pets genuinely enrich our lives with their beauty, affection, loyalty, and interactions with us.

THE PROFOUND LOYALTIES OF DOGS AND CATS

The bonds formed between pets and humans run deep. But that doesn't completely explain the lengths a dog will go to for his human. Rigorous scientific research has shown that dogs have many of the same emotional responses to their humans as a young child would have, including sympathy, empathy, and sharing emotional states. The experiments were carefully structured to discriminate between these emotions and mere canine curiosity (Coren 2012).

Do they remember us and miss us when we are away? My own experience certainly confirms it. I can especially share that my dog Jazzy has a connection with a family friend who has lived in another state for several years. When she visits, Jazzy is very excited and happy to see her, and the feelings are mutual. Jazzy will stay by her side throughout most of her visit and relish all the attention from her loving friend. It's as if she knows that she needs to soak up all the attention, as her special friend will leave once again for several months.

My experience with family pets also shows that they truly miss us when we are gone from the household. When one member of my household is away, it is as if Jazzy is on watchdog duty. Her behavior is on alert until the absent family member returns. This is followed by an exuberant reunion, with enthusiastic jumping and tail-wagging. Jazzy becomes an overflowing container of love and excitement. She is quite a jumper normally, but in moments of additional excitement, she finds it very hard to control herself as she barks, jumps, and runs back and forth with the zoomies. She then reaps all the benefits of loving physical contact, much hugging, and words of love.

Stories of dogs who have gone missing and returned to their homes are heart soothing and demonstrate how strong the human–animal bond is. Just today, I read a story of a dog missing from his home (leash and collar on the ground in the backyard) who, after many days, wandered into the store in which his owner worked.

Another happy ending occurred when three-year-old Max backed out of his collar on a walk and just took off. Fortunately, he survived on his own, lost in the woods for almost a year. After searching and posting on social media, his family saw a post about a dog sighting. Max was caught by Lost Paws Trapping. Max and his family had a very emotional reunion, and his family is grateful for the happy ending (CBS News 2017).

When we are alive and with our pets, we share a special devotion. That devotion often remains after death. In 2011, a Navy SEAL's beloved dog, Hawkeye, lay at the foot of the casket, lying in vigil throughout the funeral ceremony (Ng 2011). In 2018, former US president George H. W. Bush's service dog, Sully, was at vigil before his casket during the various services for the deceased president (National Public Radio 2018).

The remarkable story of a dog named Hachiko is a shining example of a dog with a never-ending loyalty to his owner. This particular true story took place in Japan in the 1920s and 1930s and is a powerful example of the very special attachment that can exist between a dog and its owner.

Hachiko, an Akita, was born in 1923 and made his home with a professor at Tokyo Imperial University (King 2014). Every day Professor Ueno walked to the train station and boarded the train to the university for a day of work. Hachiko, his faithful companion, would accompany him on the daily walk to the train station and return later to meet the professor for his return home. After following this routine for several years, a day came when Professor Ueno did not return to the train station. Unfortunately, Professor Ueno had suffered a sudden cerebral hemorrhage that ended his life. His faithful dog, Hachiko, continued to wait for him at the train station day after day, at the exact time he was due to arrive. He waited every day for nine years. It didn't matter if there was rain, snow, or sunshine, he always went back to wait at the exact time his train was due to arrive. The regulars at the train station found out what happened to Professor Ueno, and began to take charge of feeding and taking care of Hachiko. His loyalty to his owner earned him the nickname "the faithful dog" from many people in Japan.

Hachiko died at the train station in 1935, after nine years of faithfully waiting for Professor Ueno's return from work. Soon after Hachiko's death, a statue of him was erected outside the Shibuya train station in Tokyo. In 2015, a statue of Professor Ueno and Hachiko was unveiled at the university where Professor Ueno taught. This faithful dog never gave up, and he touched the hearts of many people of Japan and became their hero. People from all over the world visit these statues. They serve as a symbol of a dog's never-ending love and devotion and speak to the strength of the human–animal bond.

Our pets can also come to our rescue. One cold October night, a husband and wife were sleeping in their house in Montana. Schnautzie the cat ambled onto the wife's chest and then greeted her with numerous taps to her nose with her paws. The sleeping woman initially viewed it as just an adorable annoyance in the night and ignored it. However, Schnautzie the cat was persistent and continued *tap . . . tap . . . tap*. She then noticed that Schnautzie was conspicuously sniffing the air. She woke her husband, and they noticed a hissing noise. It turned out that a gas pipe leading into their home had broken and was filling their basement with fumes. The couple and their cat fled the house and made it to safety. A firefighter told them later that if the furnace had kicked on during that cold night, the whole house could have exploded in flames. The family credits their cat, Schnautzie, with saving their lives (Coffey 2014).

Recognition of the Bond in Recent Laws

After the Hurricane Katrina disaster, with many people working to advocate on behalf of people and their pets, a law was enacted in 2006 titled the "Pets Evacuations and Transportation Standards" (PETS) Act. This act had near unanimous support and ensures that pets in natural disasters will not be separated from their families. The law requires rescue agencies to save pets as well as their people. This was not the case during Hurricane Katrina. This law was a turning point in our relationships with cats and dogs, marking when they became legal members of society.

Hurricane Katrina was the pivotal moment in our history for us and our pets. Now there is more recognition that pets should be treated as members of our families. Charlotte Bass Lily, a well-known animal activist, was heavily involved in the post-Katrina animal rescue operation. Several other volunteer groups working with Bass Lily helped save over eight thousand animals affected by that natural disaster. David Grimm, author of the book *Citizen Canine: Our Evolving Relationship with Cats and Dogs*, pointed out a very important finding after speaking with Charlotte Bass Lilly. Charlotte conveyed this message to him when she said, "I don't think the world realized what pets meant to people before Katrina." She then added, "Now they know there's a human–animal bond that can't be broken" (Grimm 2014).

We already knew that our pets are a special part of our lives, but this new law validated that our pets are truly members of our society. History tells us that our cherished pets evolved from being wild creatures over thousands of years to become working animals, pets, and companions. More recently, there is recognition that they are members of our families, sharing our homes. Our pets have a special place in our homes and in our hearts, and our hearts ache when they leave this world. It is no wonder we intensely mourn their loss. If there were doubts about how much people care for their pets, the aftermath of Hurricane Katrina helped us realize just how much.

Many years after Katrina, my son Steven helped to staff one of the local shelters in my area where people were sheltered as Hurricane Sandy was looming. Knowing that it would be of great interest to me, he shared that several shelters were specifically set up to accept pets with their families for the duration of this storm and its aftereffects. Local animal welfare groups supplied food and bedding for the pets, and they were able to be with their family members to weather the storm together. This was a further testament that the human–animal bond will not be broken. The unfortunate disaster of Hurricane Katrina was truly a pivotal point in our history and cast the light brightly on the human–animal bond of love.

How lucky for us that we have these magnificent animals with whom we can share life!

Recognition of the Bond by Employers: Bereavement Leave for Our Pets

Given the significance of the bond we share with our pets, and how the loss affects us so much, it seems odd that this is not widely recognized by employers as a valid loss but becomes a "disenfranchised" one. Sadly it is not, largely because many have never experienced the bond people have with their pets. Frequently this loss cannot be spoken about openly at work without risking feelings of shame or embarrassment. Coworkers who do not validate your feelings can make for a difficult return to work if you have not been given sufficient time to work through your feelings. You may feel that if you were to have an outburst of sadness during the workday, it would be accompanied by a lack of understanding from your coworkers. You may even expect to receive the unhelpful suggestion that you should be "over this," as it was "only" a [dog, cat, bird].

We may want to ask for time off from work, just as we would take time off for a human death in our lives. Even feeling a little bit supported would be helpful. However, we frequently do not, because our society has no established traditions associated with pet loss, like it does for the loss of a human family member. Sometimes we may feel that others are judging us negatively for not recovering quickly. We may feel we cannot fully share how much this loss impacts us. When we grieve the loss of a pet, one of the last things we want to worry about is work and whether we can take time off to help us grieve our loss. How can we manage to go into work dealing with the very raw feelings of our grief?

The good news is that some companies now offer pet bereavement leave (CBS News 2016). Recognition of this loss by an employer can go far in terms of employee satisfaction and retention, as well as goodwill from employees toward their employer. It also makes the point with one's coworkers that this loss matters.

Many individuals might have never experienced a bond with a pet and may fail to realize the importance of this grief and the impact it can have on one's life. It is important for employees to feel they are supported by their coworkers and places of employment. Perhaps employers can consider other options that employees can use during this difficult time, including flex time, remote work, and flexible work schedules. These can go a long way in making employees feel that they are valued and their loss is indeed validated. The creation of a work environment where employees feel valued can have positive outcomes for all in the workplace.

REFLECTIVE WRITING EXPERIENCES

CHAPTER 1:

The Human-Animal Bond
Writing Experience—All About Your Special Pet

Write about one or more of these topics in your notebook:

- Why was this name chosen for your pet?
- What were all the other names or ways you addressed your pet?
- What was their favorite food or snack?
- How did you feel the first time you saw this pet and why?
- What were their physical characteristics (color, breed, size, etc.)?
- What was your daily or weekly routine with your pet?
- What special activities did you do together?
- Was there a special place your pet liked to hang out?
- What were some of their silly antics?
- Did your pet have another animal buddy?
- If so, what did the other pet look like and what did they do together?
- Was there a special time you especially looked forward to and interacted with your pet (when you played ball or Frisbee together or cuddled on that particular chair, for example)?

"Clearly, animals know more than we think, and think a great deal more than we know."

—IRENE M. PEPPERBERG

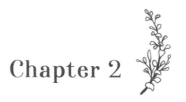

Chapter 2

Pets, Humans, and Their Health Together

aving a pet in your life provides many rewarding benefits, such as improved physical health, better emotional well-being, and enhanced social support. These animals truly are our healing helpers. Besides the healing help, they provide us with unlimited unconditional love. Is there any wonder, then, that we grieve intensely when they leave this world, or when we otherwise lose them?

Our pets and companion animals are indeed our healing helpers. As you read, perhaps it will help you to think about the specific ways your pet has healed and helped you, and those thoughts will help you to celebrate their life with you. I encourage you to reflect on how they have had a positive impact on your own life and the lives of others who have engaged with them.

Animals have a long history of healing us. Very early in our history we can find accounts of the therapeutic value of animals. While ancient accounts of human–animal interaction in history are a bit sparse, it was generally believed that animals could contribute to a person's well-being. In modern times, researchers are rigorously proving the very real benefits of animals in our lives. Thankfully, the good news is that we now have the research to back up the early anecdotal accounts, and it conclusively shows the very real benefits of animals in our lives. Whether they have a job as a service animal or serve as our companion animal ("pet"), we can definitely show the wonderful ways our lives have been enriched by animals.

Pet parents intuitively know that living with a pet comes with many benefits, including constant companionship, love, and affection. We can also gain a different kind of well-being from our companion animals in the way of physical health benefits. Rigorous documentation has shown that animals offer an array of health benefits beyond their loving companionship. During the 1980s and 1990s, hunches and observations turned into research and documentation. Alan Beck, ScD, and Aaron Katcher, MD, a psychiatrist at the Center for the Human–Animal Bond at Purdue's School of Veterinary Medicine, cowrote *Between Pets and People: The Importance of Animal Companionship*, in which they cited a 1992 study of five thousand people that revealed that pet owners had lower blood pressure and blood fat levels than non–pet owners (Beck and Katcher 1996).

Here are some other statistics showing the health benefits of pets. People living with dogs are 15 percent less likely to die from heart disease (Shmerling 2018). Pet owners have higher one-year survival rates following heart attacks than do non–pet owners, and pet ownership, particularly dog ownership, may lower the risk of cardiovascular disease. Multiple studies indicate that pets are a powerful form of stress relief, lowering not only blood pressure but also harmful stress hormones like cortisol, which is associated with depression and anxiety. They also increase beneficial hormones like oxytocin, which is linked to happiness and relaxation. Additionally, some people experience increased output of endorphins and dopamine after just five minutes with a dog (Beck and Katcher 1996).

The animals in our lives can provide other noted health benefits, as noted here:

* Pet ownership was associated with a reduced risk for non-Hodgkin lymphoma and diffuse large B-cell lymphoma (Trahan et al. 2008).

* Human health savings of $3.86 billion over ten years have been linked to pet ownership as related to a decrease in doctor visits in studies in Austria and Germany (Heady et al. 2002).

* A therapy dog has a positive effect on patients' pain level and satisfaction with their hospital stay following total joint arthroplasty (Harper et al. 2014).

* Fibromyalgia patients who spent time with a therapy dog instead of alone in an outpatient waiting area at a pain management facility showed significant improvements in pain, mood, and other measures of distress (Marcus et al. 2013).

* A walking program that matched sedentary adults with therapy animals resulted in an increase in walking over a fifty-two-week graduated intervention, with participants saying they stuck with the program because "the dogs need us to walk them" (Johnson and Meadows 2010).

* Animals also serve people during wartime. The United States Army Medical Department Journal (AMDJ) mentions cavalry horses, sentry dogs, carrier pigeons, and even animals in the role of mascots as common historical military roles for animals. According to the AMDJ, these animals not only provided protection but also offered stress relief and a sense of pride to their human counterparts (Lenhard 2018).

* Not only are people physically healthier in the presence of animals; they're mentally healthier and happier too. In a 2016 survey of pet owners conducted by the Human–Animal Bond Research Institute (HABRI), 74

percent of pet owners reported mental health improvements from pet ownership, and 75 percent reported that a friend's or family member's mental health had improved from pet ownership (Human–Animal Bond Research Institute 2016).

Pets also can offer benefits for other human health challenges. The elderly respond well to companion animals. Many conditions like depression, coronary heart disease, and dementia can be exacerbated by the loneliness that elders face in their daily lives. By interacting with companion animals, elderly people can experience positive mental and physical effects, and similar results can occur in children as well.

Let's not forget that even though the four-legged furry friends sometimes get all the credit, other pets can help us too. Watching a fish tank for a period of time instead of a bare wall can lower our blood pressure and can be seen as a powerful relaxant similar to meditative techniques (University of Exeter 2015).

The human–animal bond can be observed in a variety of settings. Working animals are especially known for their relationships with their human handlers. For example, emotional support, therapy, and service animals provide comfort, offer security, and perform daily tasks to help their owners through life. Animals can be an important part of the healing process for people who experience abuse or trauma, including veterans who have served during wartime.

ANIMALS AND CHILDREN

The interaction and connection that children can experience by being with a pet has no price tag. The many lessons a pet can teach children have a valuable impact upon their lives. It's no wonder we welcome them into our lives. Even young children can start learning how to be responsible and accountable for their pet's needs by being in charge of checking their water bowl and filling it when it's low. Pets can help children learn nurturing skills that transfer to their human families. For example, when their pet seems out of sorts, they may soothe them by talking quietly with them and rubbing their tummy. When the child is not feeling well, their pet will most likely sense that and provide extra cuddle time. Pets offer children a listening, nonjudgmental ear; they never criticize what they hear and never ever repeat it. What a great confidant! Pets in children's lives provide laughter, joy, many stories to share, and memories to cherish. A child's pet can teach about the circle of life. It is no small wonder that they leave a huge mark on our lives, and when the bond is broken through their death, we grieve deeply.

Here are some additional documented positive effects that companion animals have upon children:

- 🐾 The presence of an animal can significantly increase positive social behaviors among children with disorders on the autism spectrum (O'Haire et al. 2013).

- 🐾 Children made fewer errors in match-to-sample categorization tasks in the presence of a dog, compared with a stuffed dog or a human (Gee, Church, and Altobelli 2010). Similar studies may indicate that the presence of a dog serves as both a source of motivation and a highly salient stimulus for children, allowing them to better restrict their attention to the demands of the task (Gee et al. 2015).

- 🐾 Therapy animals in pediatric cancer studies improved motivation to participate in treatment protocols, to maintain motivation over time, and to want to "get better" or stay optimistic (Sobo, Eng, and Kassity-Krich 2006, Barker and Wolen 2008).

SOCIAL BENEFITS

Our pets boost our self-esteem, as they don't judge or criticize us. For the lonely or elderly, they provide companionship, love, and sometimes a purpose in life.

Dogs, as well as other animals with whom we engage, help us to socialize more and may well serve as an introduction. If we are at a dog park or out for a walk with our dog, we might be more inclined to offer a greeting to our neighbors.

PHYSICAL HEALTH: MORE THAN AN EXERCISE MACHINE

Our pets can be great teachers of the benefits of physical activity. Additionally, participation in physical activity increases as our pets (especially dogs) urge us to take them for walks, and show us the importance of a good stretch. They remind us to be playful (my Jazzy picks up a ball in her mouth and walks up to me, and I certainly take the hint), live life to the fullest, and be in the present moment. Benefits of play with our pet can include strengthening our bond with them, providing mental stimulation and physical exercise, and relieving stress. These benefits go to both you and your pet. Not to mention, it can be pure fun!

Many of the benefits to our physical health go beyond what would be expected from the additional physical exercise alone:

🐾 A 2013 report in *Circulation* by the American Heart Association describes a strong relationship between pet ownership and mitigation of risk factors for cardiovascular disease, including increased physical activity, better lipid profiles, reduced stress, and better survival rates after an acute cardiovascular issue (American Heart Association 2013).

🐾 In England, Cambridge University researchers discovered that within *only a month* of taking a cat or dog into their homes, new owners reported highly significant reductions in minor ailments (Sakson 2009).

🐾 Notable physical health benefits of the pets in our lives include a decrease in blood pressure. Studies have shown that interacting with pets through the simple acts of petting and talking to them helps to lower pulse rate and blood pressure. For example, a study of six thousand patients at the Baker Medical Research Institute in Melbourne, Australia, revealed that people with pets had lower blood pressure, lower cholesterol, and lower risk of heart attack (Sakson 2009). Some reasons for these results are that animals help reduce our state of arousal. They also have a steady presence and provide us with many opportunities to both give and be the recipients of the basic human need for touch. Even if having a pet reduces your blood pressure or cholesterol, do not stop medication without consulting your doctor.

EMOTIONAL HEALTH AND WELL-BEING

Our pets also substantially help our emotional health and well-being. They offer no judgment and can be great listeners. They pick up on our emotions; whether you are in the company of a dog, cat, rabbit, or hamster, talking to them can be very useful. The act of simply saying things aloud can help you to work through your thoughts. I can attest to this, as I talk to my dog, Jazzy, all the time, and she really seems to listen in her own special way and to snuggle more as she senses my needs. Sometimes when we cuddle and she is on my lap, she faces out, and then there are the times she is on my lap and facing me. It is then when I know I have her attention, because she makes eye contact, raises her small perfect triangular-shaped ears, and gently tilts her head when I speak to her. I feel a strong connection to her, and a calm feeling comes over me. I believe she is there for me in her own special way and wants me to feel better.

As pet parents, we have on numerous occasions been the recipients of the feel-good hormones produced in our bodies by interacting with our pets. They have helped us reduce the stress that is common in our everyday lives. Meg Daley Olmert, in her book titled *Made for Each Other—The Biology of the Human–Animal Bond*, writes about the hormone oxytocin (Olmert 2009). This chemical flows through and between all mammals and inspires us to connect with others. It is best known as the hormone that causes labor and lactation in nursing moms. Regardless of age or gender, we all produce it and we all need it. When we interact with the animals in our lives, it becomes capable of relieving stress. Scientists have learned of its powerful effects in human–animal relationships, and research shows that oxytocin levels almost always double in both people and dogs when humans talk to and stroke their pets.

Interacting with your pet can also help you relax, ease tension, and even relieve physical pain. Sometimes, we may even say that our best therapists have fur and four legs, or maybe they have fins or feathers. Sometimes they are exactly what we need to put a positive spin on our day and help us be in the present moment.

REFLECTIVE WRITING
EXPERIENCES

CHAPTER 2:

Pets, Humans, and Their Health Together
Writing Experience—Pets Enhance Our Health

How has your pet enhanced your health or helped you heal during your life together? Did your pet's need for a daily walk encourage you to start a daily walking program? Did your pet help ease your anxiety with their loving presence and all the cuddling moments? Think about some specific ways your pet has brought healing and health into your life. Take out your notebook, close your eyes, and take some deep soothing breaths. Begin to recall all the ways your pet may have helped you through any health concerns. Let the words gently flow from your heart and mind with gratitude for your pet's presence in your life.

"They bring us love and happiness and comfort without end.
It's hard to face such sadness without your furry friend."

—UNKNOWN

Chapter 3

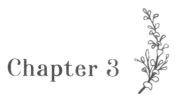

Healing Companionship
of Pets

his chapter traces the healing companionship of pets, from early anecdotal records to contemporary accounts. It highlights, with many examples, the remarkable abilities of animals who have made a difference in our lives. This chapter brings us full circle to how animals have made significant contributions to the quality of our lives. The loss of our cherished pets impacts us in many profound ways, and the hurt we suffer can be overpowering. Reflecting upon the magnitude of their interactions throughout time can help us to come to a fuller understanding of why their loss hurts so much. Let us honor all the important times they have been there to help us throughout history.

EARLY ANECDOTAL RECORDS

As far back as the ninth century, there are records citing animals assisting the disabled. Rabbits and chickens were parts of therapies for mentally ill individuals. Records of pets as therapeutic agents date back to 1699, when John Locke, an English physician, advocated "giving children dogs, squirrels, birds, or any such thing as to look after as a means of encouraging them to develop tender feelings and a sense of responsibility for others" (Fine 2015).

In 1867, farm animals, especially horses, supported epilepsy patients in their therapy at Bethel Epilepsy Center in Bielefeld, Germany. Bethel is now a five-thousand-patient treatment facility for mental and physical disorders. Many animals, including dogs, cats, birds, and horses, are still part of the treatment program at Bethel (Salotto 2001).

The York Retreat was established by the Quakers (Salotto 2001). This facility has the distinction of having been the first establishment in England where mental illness was regarded as something from which a person could recover, and patients were treated with sympathy, respect, and dignity. Individuals at the facility would care for small animals in the hope that this would provide them with the opportunity to learn such things as self-control. Unfortunately, there was not widespread acceptance at that time that animals could improve psychological issues. However, anecdotal evidence did suggest that animals were at least helpful.

Later in the nineteenth century, Florence Nightingale observed that small pets relieved depression, especially in patients with chronic illness (Fine 2010). This began a wave of informal experiments involving animal interaction with humans to produce a calming effect on patients suffering from anxiety.

HEALING HELPERS IN THE EARLY TWENTIETH CENTURY

During the early twentieth century, our healing helpers rendered invaluable assistance during the deadly outbreak of diphtheria in Nome, Alaska, in the winter of 1925 (Reamer 2020). Many more lives would have been lost if the valued serum from Nenana, over six hundred miles away, had not been delivered in time. Public health officials knew the only way to obtain the lifesaving serum would be to use dog sleds. A relay of twenty teams was assembled with their mushers, and amazingly in just *five days*, the prototype Iditarod was completed and the lifesaving serum delivered. Many dog teams were part of this relay, but two of the lead dogs have become famous for their roles in the serum run. Balto was the lead dog on the fifty-three-mile final leg, but Togo and his musher traversed 264 miles through extremely treacherous conditions. It was truly a team effort, and Balto and Togo, dogs that were truly "healing helpers," have received much special recognition for their roles in it.

TWENTIETH-CENTURY THERAPEUTIC ANIMALS

In the United States, animals were first used therapeutically in the 1940s at a US Air Force convalescent hospital in New York City (Levinson 1997). Animals were used at this site to promote the patients' well-being, by allowing them to observe, care for, and touch the animals. Sponsored by the American Red Cross, this program used dogs, horses, and farm animals as a diversion from the intense therapeutic programs the airmen underwent. Unfortunately, no detailed records can be found, and after the war, the program was discontinued.

In the late 1950s, Boris Levinson, a psychology professor at Yeshiva University in New York City, was working with a withdrawn and uncommunicative child (Salotto 2001). His dog, Jingles, was at his feet in his office when mother and child arrived a few hours early for their appointment. When they entered his office, Jingles greeted the child and immediately established rapport with the child. The child showed no fright at all. When the mother tried to separate child and dog, Dr. Levinson motioned to her to let them be. For the first several sessions, the child was primarily involved with Jingles, but Dr. Levinson was able to gradually include himself in their conversations. After a while, he and the child were able to work on the issues, and he made substantial progress in resolving them. Dr. Levinson gave a lot of credit to Jingles as a willing co-therapist in later accounts of his work with this client. Levinson's original paper was presented at a meeting of the American Psychological Association in 1961. He later published a book, *Pet-Oriented Child Psychotherapy*, in 1969. This book is based on his discoveries in his psychotherapy practice with Jingles and his clients. He later referred to this as "pet therapy." It is now referred to as "pet-assisted therapy," "animal-assisted therapy," or even "animal-facilitated therapy."

Current interest in the value of companion animals to human health was generated in large part by this work, as well as the work of Samuel and Elizabeth Corson. However, this work was not taken seriously until Freud's experiences with his own dog, Jofi, came to light (Fine 2010).

Investigators in the field have newly discovered that psycho-analyst Sigmund Freud frequently had his dog, Jofi, in his office with him, even during psychotherapy sessions. Jofi was originally a personal comfort to him, as he claimed that he felt calmer when Jofi was in the room with him. However, Freud soon began to notice that the presence of his dog seemed to help his clients as well. Freud's views on animals' therapeutic potential did not become widely known until almost two decades after his death, when a series of books were released that included translations of his professional letters and journals.

CONTEMPORARY ANIMAL HELPERS

The positive effects of animal-assisted interventions are available more now than ever before, as they become increasingly popular and as researchers continue to rigorously verify and document the benefits of pets in our lives. In a survey during 1971, psychotherapist Boris Levinson found that one-sixth of New York psychotherapists included pets in their treatments (Alliance of Therapy Dogs 2017). Today animals are becoming increasingly popular as co-therapists in mental health treatment, in remedial education, in rehabilitation work in prisons, and even as emotional support animals for students during exams.

Also in the 1970s, the Delta Foundation, later known as the Delta Society, was founded as a clearinghouse for research involving animal-assisted intervention. In 1981, it added the human–animal bond to its mission. In 2012, The Delta Society formally changed its name to Pet Partners. Utilizing research from the 1980s and 1990s, Pet Partners produced the first comprehensive standardized training for animal-assisted activities and therapy for health-care volunteers and health-care professionals.

Some specific examples of helping animals are discussed below.

Service Dogs and Other Animals

Service animals are animals trained to assist people with disabilities with the activities of normal living. They have very specific training that allows them to perform certain tasks for individuals. The training is individualized for the person they will be assigned to work with, such as detecting when the person's blood sugar levels are out of balance or sniffing out an impending seizure. Most people are familiar with guide dogs for those who are blind or have other serious vision limitations. They help people feel more confident and secure when they venture out. There are also service animals who assist those who are deaf or hard of hearing, animals who alert to the presence of allergens, and even animals who provide behavior modification help to individuals with psychiatric and neurological disabilities.

All of these roles are mentioned in the Americans with Disabilities Act (ADA) definition of service animals: ". . . any . . . dog (or miniature horse) individually trained to do work or perform tasks for the benefit of an individual with a disability. Examples include, but are not limited to, assisting individuals who are blind or have low vision with navigation and other tasks, alerting individuals who are deaf or hard of hearing to the presence of people or sounds, providing nonviolent protection or rescue work, pulling a wheelchair, helping an individual during a seizure, alerting individuals to the presence of allergens, retrieving items such as medicine or the telephone, providing physical support and assistance with balance and stability to individuals with mobility issues, and helping persons with psychiatric and neurological disabilities by preventing or interrupting impulsive or destructive behaviors" (ADA National Network 2017).

The key difference between an emotional support animal (ESA) and a service animal is that a service animal undergoes in-depth training to provide a specific service to a particular individual and is allowed to go anywhere their human goes. Even though emotional support animals can be of great assistance to people, their access may be restricted.

"The Nose Knows" (Sniffer Dogs, Detection Dogs)

Sniffer dogs or detection dogs are trained dogs that use their extraordinary sense of smell to detect substances such as explosives, illegal drugs, injured and deceased humans, and many other things. There are also animals that are being trained to sniff out many types of cancers.

Dogs have an incredible olfactory capacity. They can detect odors in the parts per trillion (1 part in 1,000,000,000,000) (Castaldo 2014). This awesome ability certainly primes them to detect disease! They also have a genius for observing our behavior that helps them guide us physically and emotionally.

As this book is being written, we are in the throes of the COVID-19 pandemic, and our healing helpers have risen to the occasion. Researchers at the University of Pennsylvania are testing eight Labrador retrievers to determine whether their sensitive noses can detect the pandemic virus by scent (Fox 2020). There are widespread and wellknown instances of how we have already trained our canine friends' finely tuned noses to sniff out other deadly diseases, including malaria, diabetes, and Parkinson's. Researchers are learning that many viruses give off a unique characteristic scent. Now we can clearly understand how the nose knows!

Animal-Assisted Interventions

Animal-assisted interventions are goal-oriented, structured interventions that intentionally incorporate animals in health, education, and human services for the purpose of therapeutic gains and improved health and wellness. Animal-assisted therapy (AAT), animal-assisted education (AAE), and animal-assisted activities (AAA) are all forms of animal-assisted interventions. In all these instances, the animal may be part of a volunteer therapy animal team working under the direction of a professional, or an animal that belongs to the professional.

Animal-assisted therapy is a formal, structured set of sessions that helps people reach specific goals in their treatment. A wonderful example of animal-assisted therapy is equine-assisted psychotherapy. It involves a team approach with clients, licensed mental health professionals, and an equine specialist. Equine-assisted therapy and activities can take place on the ground or on the horse. This therapy promotes change and growth in people through activities that incorporate horses in numerous ways, such as grooming, horseback riding, and carriage driving. One great value of horses is their keen sensitivity to nonverbal communication, which enables horses to respond to a person's mood and internal emotional state. This can be helpful for people dealing with clinical problems such as depression, anxiety, and eating disorders.

Another example of animal-assisted therapy is Animal-Assisted Play Therapy®, which encourages cross-species play (child/adult and animal) in the service of therapeutic change. Appropriately trained therapists and animals engage with children and families, primarily in play interventions aimed at improving the person's psychosocial health and the animal's well-being (Van Fleet and Faa-Thomson 2017).

While animal-assisted therapy is more formal and structured, animal-assisted activities involve more casual meetings. They bring comfort and recreation to people in long-term care facilities, people receiving cancer or other medical treatment, and people dealing with anxiety. Individuals and their pets have specific training for animal-assisted therapy.

Animal-assisted education employs animals to assist in the education of children and adults. The R.E.A.D. program (discussed later in this chapter) is a wonderful example of AAE.

Emotional Support Animals

An emotional support animal (ESA) is a pet that provides therapeutic support to a person with a mental illness, as prescribed by a licensed mental health professional. The first step to either obtaining an ESA or having your current pet designated as an ESA is to discuss it with your medical or mental health professional to see if it makes sense within your current treatment plan.

Emotional support animals can be dogs, cats, or other small animals. Although they provide needed emotional support and comfort, no specific training is required, and they do not have the legal right to go everywhere with their humans. A responsible owner must provide training so they are wellbehaved. Individuals with emotional support animals do have the right to live in housing that is otherwise pet-free under the Fair Housing Act. Until a recent change, emotional support animals were allowed to accompany their owners in an aircraft cabin. As of December 2020, the Department of Transportation no longer considers emotional support animals to be service animals for purposes of flying (US Department of Transportation 2020). As a result, Alaska, American, Delta, and Southwest Airlines have banned emotional support animals from their cabins (Gilbertson 2021). It is unethical (and explicitly illegal in some states) to misrepresent a pet as an emotional support animal.

Comfort Animals

Pets have roles in hospitals, nursing homes, mental health facilities, prisons, hospices, and facilities for the physically challenged. These are known as "comfort animals" or "therapy animals" and bring much-needed support. Through their interactions with people, they provide much-needed attention and affection. They do not need any task-specific training for this role, but they do need to be calm and friendly toward new people. A good start for a dog to learn the necessary people skills would be the Canine Good Citizen training available from the American Kennel Club. Then, follow up with a therapy dog organization, such as Pet Partners or Therapy Dogs International (American Kennel Club 2020).

Comfort animals serve at funeral homes as support for those who are grieving or saying their final goodbyes to a loved one. I recently viewed a TV message about a local funeral home that now has an emotional support animal available to the grieving during funeral preparation and visitation. How comforting for many experiencing their loss to be with, interact with, and stroke a loving animal!

Pets in Educational Settings

Many colleges are responding to the stress that students experience during midterms and finals by setting up times in the student lounges where animals will be present to provide some much-needed stress relief. At some colleges, it is now possible for students to have their pet live with them on campus, especially if the pet is viewed as their emotional support animal.

The R.E.A.D. Program

Another example of a way in which our pets can help us is the Reading Education Assistance Dogs (R.E.A.D.) program, which uses therapy animals to help children improve their reading and communication skills. Dogs are brought into the classroom for an hour or two, and the children read to them, fostering a love of books and reading. First launched in Salt Lake City in 1999, it's been growing around the world. More than seven thousand therapy teams have trained and registered with the program and are going strong (Intermountain Therapy Animals 2020).

Pets in the Classroom

Pets are in our schools as classroom mascots. Classroom pets are seen as contributing to the development of compassion and responsibility for many preschool and primary school children. The classroom pet can facilitate interaction among the children and between children and adults. Many species of animals serve as classroom mascots, but it appears that fish are by far the most common. In some classrooms you may see guinea pigs, hamsters, rabbits, frogs, and toads—indeed almost any small animal.

TAILS Program in Florida

Animals play an important role in the federal, state, and local prison systems. Prisons that allow animals to visit prisoners or allow prisoners to have pets have seen a reduction in violence and improved relations between prisoners and staff. A Department of Corrections program in Florida called Teaching Animals and Inmates Life Skills (TAILS) matches at-risk dogs with institutionalized men (Jacobo 2019). The men need to qualify for the program, and it rehabilitates both the inmate and the dog for their eventual entry into society. The dogs in the program have been categorized as high-risk for being euthanized, or were seized from dogfighting, abusive, or hoarding environments. Many inmates have stated that this was the first time they felt unconditional love and the first time they were able to care for someone other than themselves. This program also teaches positive reinforcement. Inmates with children have stated that it has made them better fathers. This program offers hope for both the dogs and the men involved, and it is further confirmation of the power of our healing helpers.

Many of the above examples of helping animals can be considered animal-assisted interventions. Pet Partners is the US leader in demonstrating and promoting the health and wellness benefits of animal-assisted interventions. Since the organization's founding in 1977, the science proving these benefits has become indisputable. Its programs focus on providing direct services at the local community level. Among these initiatives is the Pet Partners® program. Pet Partners provided the first comprehensive standardized training in animal-assisted activities and therapy for volunteers and health-care professionals.

Ambassador or Greeter Dogs

On a recent vacation trip, upon entering the hotel, I was happily surprised to find a beautiful, friendly dog walking around the lobby. I thought maybe there was a dog show in town and that the dog was being checked into the hotel with his family. I soon found out that Winston was the official ambassador dog for the hotel. He was there to welcome the hotel guests and was doing an awesome job of it! It was fun to come down to the lobby and visit with him as he welcomed visitors with wide smiles on their faces. I thought, *What a great idea!*

A Few Notes on Animal Welfare

Our animal friends provide much-needed support to people in many areas. It's also very important for their handlers to ensure their welfare and well-being. For example, they need to understand animal body language and recognize the signs of animal stress before, during, and after their visits. Just like humans, these animals need regular breaks from their work and opportunities to just be themselves.

Animal welfare is increasingly protected legally. This is manifested in new laws that consider a pet's well-being, rather than treating them as mere property. For example, an addition to Alaska divorce law in 2017 made Alaska the first state in the country to require courts to take into account the well-being of a pet, and to explicitly empower judges to grant joint custody for pets. The court may award custody on the basis of what is best for the pet rather than the human owners. In the words of one of the sponsors of the bill, Liz Vazquez, "Our pets are members of our families." Pets can also be included in domestic violence protective orders. Additionally, owners of pets seized in cruelty or neglect cases are required to reimburse the cost of their shelter care (Brulliard 2017).

More recently, other jurisdictions have joined Alaska in prioritizing the welfare of our pets. For example, in 2021, a divorce court in Madrid, Spain, granted joint custody of a dog to a divorced couple. Each of the former spouses will spend a month at a time with their dog. The lawyer from the firm that brought this case to court invoked the 1987 European Union Convention for the Protection of Pet Animals. One of the things making this ruling pioneering is that the court recognized the former partners as "co-carers" instead of "co-owners." Many US states now have laws that require the courts to consider the animal's welfare in awarding custody (Schonfeld 2021). In 2021, a New York State law explicitly required courts to make those considerations. Governor Kathy Hochul said upon signing it, "For many families, pets are the equivalent of children and must be granted more consideration by courts to ensure that they will be properly cared for after a divorce." Another recent example from New York State is the bill signed into law on October 30, 2021. Among other things, it makes veterinarians mandatory reporters for suspected instances of animal cruelty and provides legal protections and privacy for them. These are similar to the mandatory reporting and reporter protections for child abuse. Upon signing the bill into law, Governor Hochul said, "To own a pet is a blessing, and we owe it to the animals of New York to keep them safe and healthy" (WHAM-TV 2021).

Bravo for these laws recognizing that pets are not mere property! Hopefully, these laws will pave the way for more laws that recognize the importance of animals in our lives. They connect with many different people and businesses, teaching them that we need to grieve for our pets when they die, just as we grieve for our human family members. We don't want to hide this loss. We want and deserve time off to grieve, and for people to recognize that we may have days that we shed some tears at work. We are not asking that others grieve as we grieve; we just want understanding and validation that others try to understand a little of what we may be going through.

RECOGNIZING WITH GRATITUDE WHAT OUR PETS DO FOR US

When we think about what we already know about how animals are healing helpers, we need to keep in mind that there is so much more that they are capable of accomplishing. There are many stories of dogs, cats, birds, rabbits, and horses in various helping roles. How lucky we are to have these precious creatures to share in our lives!

Our pets teach us more than we could have expected. We come to a fuller understanding of this as we experience them in our daily lives and in our society. The value they add to us is beyond measure as they continue to enrich our lives with their companionship, warmth, and so much more.

Even if we are not working in a formal program of animal-assisted therapy, we know we can benefit from our own pets and their impact on our mental and emotional health. Sometimes, just talking to our pets can be helpful as they cuddle on our laps or by our sides and provide us with unconditional, nonjudgmental love. We may share some of our most private thoughts with our pets as we feel their warm presence. No doubt, our loyal pets are there for us and provide us with much healing.

Let us celebrate the remarkable benefits of the interaction with our cherished pets, whatever species. Our bond is special.

REFLECTIVE WRITING EXPERIENCES

CHAPTER 3:

Healing Companionship of Pets
Writing Experience—Your Healing Companion

Looking back on this section, we can truly appreciate all of the amazing ways in which animals have helped people. Now, it's time to honor how they have helped you personally. Have they helped you by improving your physical health, enhancing your emotional well-being, or boosting your social life? Each has its own special abilities and special ways of helping you. Reflect on the many ways your pet has been a healing companion in your life. You can make a list of the many ways your pet helped heal you, such as by bringing laughter into your life, staying by your side when you felt ill, and any other way in which they were your special healer and helper.

"When those you love die, the best you can do is honor their spirit for as long as you live.

You make a commitment that you're going to take whatever lesson that person or animal was trying to teach you, and you make it true in your own life.

It's a positive way to keep their spirit alive in the world by keeping it alive in yourself."

—PATRICK SWAYZE

SECTION II

Understanding Grief and Loss

The key to coping with your grief is the knowledge and understanding presented in these four chapters.

"No matter how or when we lose our furry friends,
their love lasts a lifetime."

—UNKNOWN

Chapter 4

Adjusting to Your Loss

After the loss of a pet, a powerful physical bond has been severed. Pets can be lost in many ways, either permanently or temporarily. This chapter delves into the many ways a pet can be gone from one's life and offers compassionate insights to help.

A CHANGING BOND

The human–animal bond is a strong one. Let's keep in mind that our pet could be gone from our lives for a number of reasons. The most obvious is their death, but other issues—such as their pet parent's chronic illnesses, cancer, an unexpected accident, or a move that involves the possibility that your pet cannot be included—can also stress or break the human–animal bond. For example, members of the armed services may have periods of time when they are overseas or stationed where their pet cannot be with them. In addition, students leaving the family home for college often leave their childhood pet behind.

LOSS BY DEATH

As we mourn the death of our pet or anticipate our pet's impending death, we can come to fully appreciate what has been lost when that bond is broken. If your pet died from a sudden accident or injury, you may be experiencing traumatic shock and disbelief after witnessing what happened or upon receiving the news. You may be left with troubling questions and thoughts. Distortions in our thinking can occur, and we can experience the "what ifs" and "I should haves." ("How could this have happened? It was all my fault. I can't forgive myself. If only I didn't forget to close that gate. I didn't see him.") As a result of this trauma, you may experience physical symptoms such as shaking, headaches, stomach upsets, nightmares, and even heart palpitations. If physical symptoms continue, it may be necessary to set up an appointment with your medical professional, who can assess your symptoms and check to see if any other medical condition is generating or aggravating them.

It is difficult and sad to say, but accidents really do happen. "If only . . ." will not bring your cherished pet back. Reactions to such a loss can be very intense. You may find it difficult to find peace after what has happened. It is important to know that, after a tragic death, you may feel numb or be in a state of shock. When a tragic event or accident occurs, thinking gets cloudy. Anger and guilt may surface immediately or may simmer over time. It is of utmost importance for you to seek out and be in the presence of people who can support you through this very difficult time. Step one is to acknowledge your loss, as this is paramount to your healing and expressing your feelings. In the comfort and safety of those who care for you, who love you, and whom you trust, you can be eased onto the path of healing. Listen for different perspectives on what happened and be open to different ways of receiving help.

If you are blaming yourself for a tragic situation that claimed your cherished pet's life, search your heart and listen carefully. You know that you would never hurt your pet or put them in harm's way.

Healing begins with forgiving yourself. Think about writing a letter to your pet, and let them know you are sorry and will always love and keep them in your memory. If you remember that your beloved pet willingly gave you unconditional love and acceptance, this will help you to give yourself love and acceptance. You know that your beloved pet would not want you to continue to suffer and forgives you. The act of writing can be very therapeutic. Remember, your beloved pet was nonjudgmental.

There are many life events and circumstances that can cause you to lose your pet other than by their death. These are generally temporary but no less difficult.

Military Deployment

You just received orders that you are being deployed to a location where you cannot take your pet, and now you are faced with the sad fact that you must leave your beloved pet behind. Coming to terms with this knowledge can be heartbreaking. Knowing that you are leaving for a distant military assignment can cause much anxiety. There is so much information you probably don't have access to for this assignment, and that is immensely difficult. Military deployment may result in a short or long separation. There is a lot to consider, as you may be thousands of miles away and very hard to reach. This loss may be tempered by telling yourself that there are things in this situation that are completely out of your control. Focus on the good news. There are some things you can control, such as who may care for your pet in your absence. To help address the pain of your loss, it is best to be prepared for any number of things that can arise from this deployment. You will still miss your pet, but being prepared and making arrangements for the care of your pet in your absence will definitely help.

Here are things to consider:

Will you ask a family member or a good friend to help? A family member may initially seem like the best person, but it may later become apparent that they are not the best choice for your pet. That person may have allergies or may otherwise be physically unable to care for your active pet.

There are many responsibilities involved in caring for our pets, and it is important to consider many things before you are deployed, such as the following:

- Is my pet microchipped?

- What information will my pet's caregiver need?

This can be put into both paper and computer files. Some things to include are pictures, nicknames, favorite activities, favorite toys, snacks, family members' contacts, vet contact information, and specific health-care needs.

- Can this person manage my pet's physical needs?

- Does this person have a good relationship with my pet?

- Is this person willing to enter into a legal foster agreement?

- Can this person continue to care for and welcome my pet into their home if I do not return home?

Knowing these answers will ensure that your pet will be loved and cared for in your absence.

Service members who are facing deployment can obtain assistance from Dogs on Deployment (https://www.dogsondeployment.org/), an organization that helps members of the military needing short-term or

ADJUSTING TO YOUR LOSS | 59

long-term foster care for their pet. Another organization for military pet foster care is Guardian Angels for Soldier's Pet (https://gafsp.org/). These organizations can connect you to a network of volunteer foster homes that match pets with an appropriate caregiver. You and your special friend deserve the best hope of being reunited when you return from your deployment. Knowing you have it will definitely ease the pain of your absence.

College Student or Other Family Member Living Away

If you are a young adult who is now in college and living away from the family home, you may have deep feelings of sadness and separation anxiety. Knowing you will be separated from a pet who has been in your life for many years can be very daunting, especially when the family pet has been present since you were very young and you have a deep connection. Maybe the pet was your best friend, slept in your bed nightly, and was with you throughout your daily activities. If you can't get to see your pet very often, it can be especially difficult. I have counseled individuals in this very situation and understand how difficult this separation can be. Knowing you can control some of the situation by planning for your separation will help you with your feelings. Keep in mind that modern communication technology can now provide a virtual visit with your pet, and that may help you.

It becomes even more difficult if you were to learn that your pet's life may be coming to an end, due to advancing age or health issues. Keep the lines of communication open with your pet's primary caregivers and ask them to immediately share any news about the pet's health. If you become aware that your pet's health may become a concern, ask yourself these questions, plus any others that arise:

🐾 Do you have any special concerns or thoughts on how the death can be approached?

🐾 Do you want to be notified immediately if the pet takes a turn for the worse?

🐾 Will you try to make it home if your pet dies? If an unplanned trip home might not be possible, you might plan a future memorial service or another way to memorialize and honor the memory of your pet.

Open communication with those at home is vital to ensure a consensus on how the death will be handled. One of my clients is now making plans to speak with her family regarding her wishes to be notified immediately in the event of a decline in the health of her pet or any other significant changes in her pet's well-being. She believes engaging in the topic with her family will ease her stress and anxiety over the separation from her cherished pet.

Unplanned Necessary Move

An unplanned but necessary move can indeed cause the loss of a cherished pet. Ultimately, you may find out that you cannot bring your beloved pet with you to your new location. This loss can be heartbreaking. This relocation could be for any number of reasons, and it may result in a completely different lifestyle and a situation that would unfortunately not accommodate your pet. One example is needing to leave your home and enter an assisted living facility. You can also put some of your wishes in writing concerning your pet's care if you die before your pet. This can include information on some of the particular likes of your pet, such as favorite treats, toys, or playtime activities. This would be very beneficial if you predecease your pet, and can bring you some peace as well. A change like this can be quite difficult for your pet to cope with, and anything that can provide some continuity in their life will be beneficial.

Or perhaps you have just heard that your company is moving quite a distance from where you currently live, or maybe even to another country. Perhaps you now need alternative living arrangements because of a new or increasing physical limitation, and your new living arrangements cannot accommodate pets. This situation has much in common with the previously mentioned military deployment and family members living away. Most of the information in those earlier sections is also applicable here.

Financial Considerations

Another potential way to lose your pet is if your financial situation has markedly deteriorated to the point where you can no longer pay for veterinary care and all the other costs involved in providing a loving home for your pet. However, there are some organizations who can help pet parents obtain food and veterinary care for their pets in the event of financial concerns. Every locality is different, but I do know that some food pantries also stock pet food. When Wishbone died, a friend made a donation in his memory to an organization that provides money to pet owners who are dealing with financial difficulties. Fortunately, caring people and organizations are around, but it does take some time to find the assistance that may provide the bridge to keeping your pet with you. A good place to start is your local humane society, food pantry, or veterinarian.

Adjusting to Your Loss

Regardless of the circumstances separating you from your pet, you may experience a myriad of emotions as well as disbelief. These situations may cause stress and major adjustment issues. As previously mentioned, the first step to recovery is to acknowledge the loss and reach out to people who care and who will validate your feelings and offer you comfort. Once a situation in which you may be separated from your pet starts to unfold, you can begin to plan for the next steps. If necessary, seek out assistance from people who can help you. This is an excellent way for you to have control over at least part of the situation.

If you went on daily walks together, you may ask your neighbor if you can walk with their dog, or connect with a shelter and volunteer to walk a dog on the weekend. Focus on the beneficial activity you are engaging in with this shelter animal. This may be the only time this animal can get out today and enjoy some daylight and fresh air, and you are the one who provided that opportunity. Give yourself credit for this simple pleasure you were able to provide for this needy pet. This can be a wonderful activity to do in your pet's memory. If you were very active with your dog and went on long hikes or walks, you may wonder if you should walk down the same path. There are two ways to look at this. If it brings you strong feelings of sadness, it may be important to check out another route until the sadness becomes lighter. On the other hand, you may feel the peaceful presence of your pet on this familiar route. You are the best judge of what you can do, so follow your instincts and your heart.

Of course, there is no "grief meter," nor should there be a judgment call on someone who is grieving "more" or "less" than we think we would. Each of us has our own unique way of dealing with grief and loss. What is very important is that grief feelings need to be validated. If others are grieving too, try to understand where they are in their own individual grief and value the feeling and emotions that they need to express. When multiple family members are in grief, they can support each other. However, there are times when it can be more helpful to seek support outside the family, as everyone's emotional reserves can be depleted.

Everyone experiences loss in their own way and can respond in a variety of ways. The set of circumstances surrounding a loss is unique to each person. This is because everyone has a different relationship with their pet. It is always possible to validate what someone else is experiencing and respect another's grief. There is no right or wrong way to grieve a loss.

I wish you well as you continue on your grief journey.

REFLECTIVE WRITING EXPERIENCES

CHAPTER 4:

Adjusting to Your Loss
Writing Experience—Exploring Your Feelings, Part 1

Many feelings may be swirling around for you right now, as the death of or separation from your pet begins to impact your daily life.

It may be helpful for you to write some of these feelings down and note how they are affecting you at this moment. Through writing, we can experience the feelings of our pain and begin to release them. Writing allows us to name our feelings, acknowledge them, and slowly release them. Writing can be very therapeutic in this way. When feelings are bottled up, they can result in physical pain such as body aches. (Note that if you are experiencing body aches and pains that you did not have before this loss, it is always good to check with your physician to rule out any medical reasons for these symptoms.)

When doing this exercise, think about the feelings you are experiencing right now. Perhaps you are experiencing exhaustion, emptiness, sadness, anger, or shame. Write down your feelings on a sheet of paper or in your notebook. As you read these feelings, think of the ones that apply to you right now and circle those that are most troublesome for you. Write down next to the circled feelings whether they have become more troublesome since the passing or absence of your pet. It's okay to have these feelings; your feelings are never wrong, and they are your feelings. It is important to acknowledge them. After writing them down, sharing them with a trusted friend or family member can bring some relief. Understanding, acceptance, and validation from people you trust can help you through this. If your feelings are very disturbing to you and interfere with your daily life activities, I recommend that you consult with a professional trained and experienced in grief and loss. Section 3 (Coping with Grief) explains how to connect with a suitable mental health professional.

Writing Experience—Exploring Your Feelings, Part 2

If your feelings are very raw right now, it is even more important to express them and find some relief. Make a list of some of the feelings that have bubbled up, and explore them. Here are some possible feelings you may be encountering now or may experience later in your grief journey. You can revisit these later, add any new feelings, and make changes. The goal is to write about whatever feelings are bubbling up for you now and then express them out loud.

- I feel angry because . . .
- I feel cheated because . . .
- I feel guilty because . . .
- I feel hurt because . . .
- I feel sad because . . .
- I feel numb because . . .
- I feel shocked because . . .
- I feel [add what other feelings are coming up for you now] because . . .

Remember, sharing your thoughts and feelings with a trusted family member or friend may be helpful to help sort through and clarify them.

"Death leaves a heartache no one can heal, love leaves a memory no one can steal."

—IRISH HEADSTONE

Chapter 5

Understanding Your
Loss and Feelings

The mission of this chapter is to shed light on how the loss of a pet can impact one's life so deeply. The unique nature and strength of the human–animal bond is why the loss of a pet hurts so much. Try to seek out those who understand this loss. It is not "only a cat" or "only a dog." Your pet was a vital and important part of your life. There may be additional losses, known as secondary losses, that accompany the primary loss of the family pet, and these also need to be acknowledged and grieved. It can be especially difficult if the people in your life refuse to acknowledge your loss; this is also known as disenfranchised grief, which we will explore in a later chapter. Additionally, these losses can be complicated by links to other losses. For example, the lost pet might have been the last remaining link to a now-deceased spouse or family member.

WHY THIS LOSS HURTS SO MUCH

A pet is a family member, and when a beloved family member dies, you grieve for them. You had a one-of-a-kind relationship with them that was special and irreplaceable. Each and every pet you will ever have is unique. Someday, you may reach out to another pet with whom you can share your love, but it will never replace the cherished pet you just lost.

Grief is the normal response to a loss. Your life has changed, and there are many adjustments that come with that loss. Specifically, the loss of your cherished pet has brought about major changes in your daily life. You wake up to your pet(s) and end your day with them. You share many routines with them throughout the day that bring a sense of order and purpose to your life. Yes, these are all adjustments, but the most heartbreaking one is the fact that you no longer have the physical presence of your beloved pet.

Secondary Losses

When we are grieving the loss of a beloved pet, we may experience some additional losses. These are known as secondary or hidden losses that can occur as a consequence of the primary loss. They need to be grieved too. *Secondary* does not mean these losses are any less painful, less important, or less intense. It is important to recognize the many losses associated with the death and to grieve for each one. Here is a list of some possible secondary losses you may experience:

- ❧ The loss of unconditional love: Relationships are not simple; in fact, they can be quite complicated. Our pets are nonjudgmental and accept us for who we are. They don't care about our shortcomings or the way we look, as their love for us is unconditional. Animals live in the moment, which is wonderful, as they don't share our anxiety over the future or regrets about the past.

❧ **The loss of purpose:** Our pets are truly dependent on us, and it is easy to understand that having a pet is similar in a lot of ways to being a parent. No surprise that some family pets have been referred to as our kids. We are responsible for their lives. We ensure that they are provided with physical and emotional comfort. Many activities revolve around our animal companion's needs. We may hire pet walkers and sitters to provide our furry friend with company or exercise, if we are unable to provide these things on a consistent basis. We go to dog parks to enhance our dog's life with social activity, and we bring them on family road trips. All are efforts to provide our pets with the best care possible. Consequently, the loss of a pet can feel like the loss of a child.

❧ **The loss of a trusted friend:** Not only do our animals provide us with uninhibited emotional expression, they also allow us to express parts of ourselves that we may never let others see. They observe our weaknesses and victories, and they move through our lives with us. During times of upheaval, they often provide us with security, stability, and comfort.

❧ **The loss of routine:** Some of the routines that brought structure to your life are now gone. It is important to come to terms with the reality that your special playtime with your pet has ended, along with the special snuggle times and all the other aspects of your routine with this special pet in your life. You cannot experience these special times in the same way with any other pet, because you know this pet was one of a kind.

❧ **The loss of a primary companion:** Your pet may have been your only social companion, around whom your life revolved. Maybe there have not been any other regular close contacts in your life. Maybe you have experienced a lack of family and friends, because they have moved or died, and you relied exclusively on your pet for day-to-day support and love.

All of the above secondary losses will contribute to the primary loss of your pet and need to be acknowledged, grieved, and validated.

The loss of your pet brings an absence that can result in an empty home and a feeling of no longer being needed. We may even lose a main source of personal touch and contact if we live or spend a substantial part of our day alone. We may feel like we are not getting the attention that we desperately need and expect from this loss. We may wonder, *Why doesn't anybody understand?*

There may be others in your life who wonder why you are experiencing such intense grief, and feel that you should just get over it already. If they have never experienced a strong human–animal connection, they may feel sad for you and express some condolences, but they may also feel that you are overreacting. They may think that "It is only a dog/cat," or "You can get another one," or "Okay, your pet died recently, but don't you think you should be over this by now?" You and I know that is not the way it works. Your pet can never be replaced, as they were unlike any other presence in your life. If you are not receiving validation from others, it may be helpful to speak with them about how the loss of your pet has impacted your life. This is where it is important for you to be your own best advocate. It may be helpful to your healing to vocalize these thoughts. Use assertive communication when talking about your grief by employing "I" statements, such as "I have been very sad about the loss of my pet." If you are unsure how to begin, sharing with them some of the material in the first three chapters may be useful. You may also find these chapters helpful if you find yourself wondering about the validity of your own feelings. This is especially the case with Chapter 1, which reminds us all how close people and their pets can be. However, if it sounds like you are not going to be able to have an understanding and compassionate ear, it may be better to excuse yourself, with the possibility of coming back to it later. In this case it would be beneficial for you to follow up with yourself and write your thoughts in a journal. You can then share the experience with someone who does provide you with understanding and support. You are in control of this situation and can decide what is best for you. You know best the depths of your relationship with your cherished pet and the wonderful ways in which their life impacted yours.

Links to Other Losses

During your life, you may experience one loss at a time or a cascade of many losses close together. There are also times when the losses accumulate and add up to a very difficult period. The passing of a pet can link to previous losses of absent or deceased family members, losses of friends, or other losses. This link now compounds the loss of your pet. If these previous losses were not fully grieved and processed, they can bring more unease and difficulty to your current loss. Compounded grief can accumulate and overwhelm much later.

Indeed, in my private practice, many of my clients have shared with me that the loss of their pet can bring up a previous loss that may not have been fully grieved. I have had clients who share that the pet that died was lovingly given to them by a family member who had previously died, and when that pet died, it brought up that earlier grief. To move forward, each loss needs to be acknowledged and grieved individually. It can be like an old wound that has healed over, but a scar remains. Sometimes when you see it, a memory comes back of how the injury occurred.

Also, sometimes you don't really notice it, as it seems like it has always been there. If someone died who had been instrumental in your relationship with your now-deceased pet, and you did not grieve fully for the loss of that individual, then the death of your pet can trigger additional feelings. If that happens, this previous loss may not have been fully grieved or processed. You need to reflect on this previous loss and ensure that you have fully grieved for it. It is important to explicitly name the loss, acknowledge it, and express the feelings that arise when this loss percolates up for you. It's also important to have a support system to help you unravel some of these losses.

Processing grief is hard work, and it will take time and patience, but the healing is worth the effort. Stay with it, and little by little, the days will be a little easier to get through and the pain will soften.

REACTIONS TO GRIEF AND LOSS

You can expect to feel sadness for your loss, whether it is today, tomorrow, or years from now. Over time, the emotions soften, and coping with the loss may be less intense.

You may experience shock and disbelief. These feelings may swirl around through your head and heart before the reality hits that your wonderful pet is really gone from your life. There can even be times when you think you feel your pet's presence around you.

As we continue on this journey of grief and work through all the many emotions we may experience, we can embrace more fully all the amazing things they bring forth in us to make us a better person. They teach us so much! It is important to believe that you did what you could with what you knew at the time. Things change and evolve, and we learn new things all the time as we acquire new information. We act on what we know and believe at the time. The reality is we will always have limitations on what we can do. You wanted to do everything possible to provide the best for your cherished pet, but the reality is you have limits and can only do what you reasonably can do. We each have an inner critic; tell yourself and truly believe that you did your best in caring for your pet.

You may experience anger and regret or resentment if your pet died tragically from an accident or from intentional harm. A very traumatic experience such as an unexpected death can be devastating and may lead to trauma reactions, including nightmares, flashbacks, and intrusive thoughts. If they persist, are very intense, become unmanageable, or interfere with your daily activities for more than a few days, please reach out to a professional counselor. Severe symptoms can be an indication that you are suffering from post-traumatic stress disorder (PTSD). Symptoms that indicate possible PTSD need to be evaluated and treated by a skilled health-care provider.

These trauma reactions can be very frightening, but it is important to know that flashbacks and other symptoms can be managed. Here are some techniques or activities you can engage in *now* to help manage some of these symptoms:

- 🐾 Choose a word or phrase that brings up peace and calm for you. Silently repeat it several times as you also get in touch with your breathing. This exercise should take you back to the present rather quickly instead of farther out into more intrusive thoughts.

- 🐾 Please avoid alcohol and any drugs that are not prescribed by your doctor.

- 🐾 Connect with nature; its peaceful environment can be very comforting.

- 🐾 Surround yourself with positive people and events.

🐾 Confide in a person you can trust, as these symptoms can
be very scary to face alone.

Here is an exercise you can do to help you stay in the present
moment and alleviate runaway thoughts when you are feeling
anxious. First, prepare yourself by taking a few deep breaths.
Then look around the room for these objects; notice them and say
aloud what they are:

🐾 Five things you see around you

🐾 Four things you can touch

🐾 Three things you hear

🐾 Two things you smell

🐾 One thing you can taste

It is helpful to write this exercise down on an index card and
have it handy to use when you need it.

If your pet died after an illness, you may have strong feelings
of anger or resentment at the veterinary staff, thinking they could
have done more, though deep down you know they did everything
they could. Veterinarians are highly trained to offer compassionate care to your pet. Maybe it would be helpful to set up an appointment with your vet after some decompression time, to go
over some of your concerns and receive clarification on what
specifically happened. When your pet was in this situation, it was
a scary life-changing time for you. Feelings were elevated, and
everything may have felt very surreal. Perhaps, after some time
has passed, you may be able to revisit some of your concerns and
come to a different conclusion about the care your pet received
from the veterinary provider.

Our pets are closely intertwined with our life. We wake up to
our pets, interact with them, and conclude our day with them.

Depending on your lifestyle, they could be by your side for much of the day. They are also dependent on us. We feed them, exercise them, play with them, and care for their health. We probably spend more time with them than we spend with many other people, including our family, coworkers, and friends. Our pets see us at our best, our worst, and all points in between. They greet us when we arrive home, and have a way of melting our stress away. They continue to love us through our personal losses, and they are there with their comforting presence and love. They shower us with unconditional love and loyalty. They provide us with a sense of security and comfort. Our pets offer a source of routine and consistency in our hectic lives. This is no surprise! There is often a feeling of loneliness that follows after a furry friend dies, because of the void that results from their loss.

Lost in a Fog of Grief

Grief has a way of making us feel like we are lost or in dense fog. You may have difficulty concentrating or focusing on things. Your senses may be dulled. The routines of your life have changed, and things that seemed so important before may now seem trivial. It is common to feel exhausted, physically, mentally, and spiritually. After the initial loss, you may experience changes in your appetite and sleeping patterns. What you are experiencing may all be a part of the grieving process. It is normal. Committing to do some of the activities in Chapter 9 (Taking Care of You) can help ease some of the anxiety you may be experiencing as you process your grief.

GUILT AND FORGIVENESS

Grief manifests in a wide variety of feelings, and guilt may or may not be one of them. If guilt is a part of your grief, considering the reasons for this guilt may help to resolve it and eventually help you move forward in your grief process.

Feelings of guilt are very common when someone experiences pet loss, regardless of the cause. These feelings can be especially intense in the case of an accidental death, or if you feel that you or someone else may have inadvertently caused the death of your pet. Regardless of the circumstances, we feel responsible for our pets and may illogically blame ourselves for their death, even if we know there was nothing more we could have done. Keep in mind that you loved your pet and provided the best care you could.

Feeling guilty can set us up for endless iterations of "I should have . . ." and "If only . . . ." "I should have closed the back fence sooner tonight." "If only I had taken him to the vet sooner." While the past cannot be changed, focusing on what you may have learned from this situation that has caused you much anxiety and anguish will help you. It is about who you are *now* and things you may be willing and able to change to prevent tragedy from happening again, whether for you or for someone else. The ripple effects of what you can learn and share are immeasurable. There are so many things you will never know that might have affected the outcome. Even if you had done things differently, that does not necessarily mean that your beloved pet would not have died. Try replacing all of the "should haves" and "could haves" with "What can I do now?" Make a list of all the things in the first category on one side of the paper, and on the opposite side write the "What can I do now?" responses. Read and reflect on this, and try implementing some of your responses. Remember that you did the best you could with the information and resources you had at the time.

When we look back on any situation, there can be a tendency to continue down the road filled with regrets for how we handled it. Instead, choose to go down the road where you focus on all you did for your pet during their life. Know and accept that you would never be a part of anything that could cause their death. It is heartbreaking, but unfortunately accidents and mishaps occur in our lives.

It can be helpful to talk about your situation with somebody who is supportive of you and familiar with your loss. Express any anger or guilt you may be feeling. If you feel that you made a mistake, acknowledge it and begin to forgive yourself for it. Being compassionate with yourself may prevent guilt from overpowering you. Engaging in self-compassion can help keep the guilt in check and not allow it to take control of you. Making an apology can also help you to practice self-compassion and forgive yourself.

A good first step is to have a general discussion on the topics of guilt and grief with a trusted listener or professional counselor. That will clear the air to then get specific. Next, follow up with writing about the feelings of guilt. Finally, an actual apology can be very helpful in allowing all to experience forgiveness. An apology may help to process your feelings and gain closure if you feel responsibility for some wrongdoing. An apology can be spoken out loud or written in a letter. Direct communication can be powerful. It might be helpful to gather up all your thoughts, clarify them, and write them down before verbalizing them to others. Then you can get together those involved and talk at a convenient time and place.

The six elements of apologies to both you and others may be helpful to resolve any guilt you may be feeling (Association for Psychological Science 2016). The text after each element are examples to illustrate a specific scenario and relate them to pet loss:

1. **Expression of regret:** I am sorry that my actions caused our pet to escape from the yard.

2. **Explanation of what went wrong:** A lock instead of a simple latch can help prevent this from happening again.

3. **Acknowledgment of responsibility:** It was not my intent to cause our pet to be injured; this was a very serious oversight on my part, and I realize the seriousness of what happened as a result of my actions and the impact it had on your life.

4. **Declaration of repentance:** What I did was avoidable, and I will make it a point to close the gate correctly and not be in a rush to move on to the other parts of my day.

5. **Offer of repair:** An actionable step now can translate to answering this question: What can I do to make amends? Giving to an organization by volunteering to help other animals in various ways can be something you might do in recognition of the pet that was injured or died. I can buy a lock for the gate instead of just having the latch. If I install a lock, the extra time it takes to secure it can make this unfortunate event not happen again. I can also pay for a trainer to work with our pet and learn some common commands that might prevent something similar from happening. If you don't feel the ideas I presented are helpful, I would be willing to do something else that you might suggest that may be helpful.

6. **Request for forgiveness:** Express your sorrow that this incident happened and caused a major impact on their life and yours. Speak in a calm tone and be gentle. It's important to recognize that the other person's response may not be what you are hoping to receive; they may not be ready to forgive. Should that happen, you need to be ready to move on.

A study by Roy Lewicki of Ohio State University and colleagues found that the most important component is item 3, "Acknowledgment of responsibility." Conversely, item 5, "Offer of repair," may not be useful or appropriate when a death has occurred. Depending on circumstances, while a life cannot be brought back, an "offer of repair" could be something like helping others to avoid the mistakes you may feel guilty about, by educating them about your experience. For example, if you attend a support group for pet loss, you could share your experience surrounding this loss and any thoughts on how you might make some changes to prevent that type of accident from happening again.

Learn from Mistakes in the Face of Guilt

Learning from a mistake can go a long way to assuage guilt. If you made a mistake, you can learn from it. We all make them. You can allow them to become positive forces, or allow them to fester within you.

Find Something Positive

If you have an accidental loss, choosing to find a way to bring out something positive from it can be very helpful to your healing. As difficult as it is to go through a sudden tragic loss, you can find a way to bring out something positive. Please realize that any mistakes that may have been made were not made with bad intentions. It may be helpful to first focus on all the good care and love you gave your pet during their life. Then focus less on what went wrong. We can get stuck in the endless cycle of blaming ourselves and ignoring the part of ourselves that forgives and is open to healing. Forgiveness of yourself and others allows healing to happen. Extend compassion to yourself (and others if they were involved in an accident) in the same way that you extended compassionate care for your pet throughout their life. Forgiveness takes practice, and you are deserving of it. Focusing on positives can offer a much-needed respite to you now. This is not intended to minimize a difficult loss, but refocusing on all the positives the pet brought to you will help.

Be Compassionate with Yourself

Even though you are reeling from guilt, you still need to be compassionate with yourself. Forgiving yourself is a major part of self-compassion. The process of forgiving yourself can begin by accepting what happened, learning and growing from the experience, and allowing yourself to move forward. Forgiveness is a choice.

Give Yourself Some Time

Each emotion you are feeling needs to be addressed. It may take a long time to work through these feelings. You have been through a lot since you embarked on this grief journey. It is very important to continue to be in contact with the people who care about you and who can continue to acknowledge and validate your loss and support you through it. When reflecting on your guilt, talk it through in a safe place with people that you know will listen without judging.

FINDING SUPPORT THROUGH YOUR GRIEF

Here are some things to consider when finding support through your grief. You have choices. I have lost precious pets and been filled with grief. It was difficult to have them leave this earth and my life. Their memories live on in my heart, and I remain grateful that they were in my life.

You may not believe that losing a cherished pet can bring us as much or even more grief than the death of a human family member. *How could this possibly be the case?* you ask. Consider our complicated relationships with others. Life brings many changes, and loved ones unfortunately die, friendships end, children leave home, and a spouse or partner may no longer be in one's life. Our pets remain through the many changes in our lives until they are no longer with us. Our relationships with human beings are needed, wanted, and certainly valued, but we also want our relationships with our pets to be valued at the same level as our relationships with human beings.

In my practice, I work with individuals, families, and groups experiencing anguish over the loss of their pets, as well as numerous other grief issues. If you decide to contact a professional counselor, you could check with them to determine whether they have experience or interest in counseling people through pet loss grief. When some of my clients reached out to schedule an appointment, they wanted to ensure that I could truly understand how this loss was impacting their lives before deciding to meet with me. They had just lost their beloved pet and were searching for a counselor who would really understand that pets are members of the family and that our bond with them is very strong. They asked me a few questions to make sure that I was that person. You can do the same. Don't be afraid to ask a prospective counselor if they have experience with pet loss. The counselor will appreciate knowing in advance why you want to meet with them.

What can we do when we are surrounded by people who minimize our loss, devalue it, and feel that we are overreacting? We can choose to be with people who truly understand our loss. If this support is not available through a family member or friend, there may be support groups for pet loss in your area. Connecting with others who have lost cherished pets can be helpful for many; as you share your story and receive feedback, you will feel that your loss is important. You may also wish to seek assistance from a qualified and experienced grief and loss counselor with a special interest in helping people through the loss of a pet. In my professional work with people who are grieving the loss of their pet, some prefer sharing their story one-on-one with me. Sometimes, clients have started out in a one-on-one counseling relationship and then moved on to a group.

There is no denying that a loss of a pet is heartbreaking and one you wish you would never have to endure. It is the price for loving! You may have a lot of raw emotion right now, if your loss is recent. Or perhaps it is an unresolved loss that needs some tender loving care. After you work through some of the very difficult feelings of your loss and come to a better understanding and eventually acceptance, you can once again embrace living more freely and not be afraid to love again. A quote by the English poet Alfred, Lord Tennyson, is highly relevant and speaks to this loss in your life: "'Tis better to have loved and lost than never to have loved at all."

You Are Not Alone

Grief is a normal response to a loss. It can show up in various ways for us and can affect us physically, cognitively, behaviorally, socially, and spiritually. The process of grief includes acknowledging your loss, coping with your loss, and expressing your loss in ways that help you to release the resulting feelings in a healthy manner. Working through the many parts of your grief process can help you come to terms with the reality of this loss, and there is no one way to go through this process. You can get through this grief, and there is no timeline for it. There are others either inside or outside of your circle who can help.

I am hoping you now fully know that you do not have to go through it alone. I hope you are finding some comfort in knowing that you can reach out to someone who has experienced this type of grief, whether a family member, good friend, grief counselor, faith leader, or grief support group. There are also hotlines that you can call for assistance; I have listed some in Appendix B.

If you are worried about how you feel, or if these feelings are interfering with your life, it is time to reach out for help. I understand that reaching out for outside help can be difficult, and even a bit scary, but talking with a trained counselor who specializes in grief and loss can help you find effective ways to cope with this very special loss. This kind of support is different from talking with a trusted friend or family member and can be critical if you are experiencing thoughts and feelings that are interfering with your daily life.

You Will Get Through This

It is vital that you try not to suppress your feelings. Sometimes you may not even realize that you are doing this, as it may have become a long-standing pattern in your life. It is possible that you have minimized or suppressed your feelings for a long time. When we suppress our feelings, it's as if we put them in a box and close the lid. It seems to work for a while . . . maybe . . . until the box becomes full, and they spill out everywhere. Suppressing and not releasing your feelings can manifest in your body in many forms, including physical aches and pains. You may feel a little apprehensive about sharing your feelings, and I realize that can be challenging. However, try to attend to these feelings, as it should ease some of them and make them more manageable. Start out slowly, and release some pieces of how you feel by naming and acknowledging them out loud. As you feel more comfortable, you can share some of your feelings with a trusted friend. It is important to express them and to understand that what you are feeling is important and needs to be heard. Your grief is unique to you, and you don't need to make any apologies for it. You have suffered a terrible loss upon losing your pet, and you deserve to grieve in your own way and on your own timeline. You will get through this. It is possible. I know, because I have experienced it too. I know from my own personal experience that it is very hard, and, at times, it seems insurmountable. Please, reach out to someone who understands and validates what you are feeling. The life you had with your beloved pet will always be in your heart and memories, and they cannot be taken away from you.

I hope this chapter has shed light on why the relationship you have with your pet is special and unique, and how such a loss can impact your life so deeply. Go forward with confidence, and know that you can feel better and move through your grief journey with more understanding, knowing that healing can take place in your life.

REFLECTIVE WRITING EXPERIENCES

CHAPTER 5:
Understanding Your Loss and Feelings

Before beginning, it may be helpful to review the general instructions for reflective writing experiences.

Writing Experience #1—Write a Letter to Your Pet

Reflect on your life together with your dear pet. What are some things you wish you could say to your pet now if they were here? (*I enjoyed playing ball with you, you were my best friend, and I miss you so much.* You get the idea.) Don't worry about grammar, spelling, or anything else except expressing what is in your heart. This can be a very healing experience that I hope you will try, as it can allow you to have a release of emotions. Yes, it's okay to cry.

Writing Experience #2—Your Pet Writes a Letter to You

If your pet could tell you some things, it would be very interesting and very helpful. Unfortunately, they can't, but you know your pet well, so you are assigned to write this letter. Relax and reflect on your life together. Your beloved pet has now passed on. I bet your pet will tell you what a great life they had with you and some of the favorite activities they did with you. Focus on all the wonderful times you had together. Again, don't worry about grammar, spelling, or anything else except expressing what is in your heart. No one needs to see this unless you choose to share it. It can be saved and reread again at another time. It can help you to focus on the positives, and allow all the good feelings and memories to surface. Focusing on the positives can produce endorphins (the "feel-good" hormones) in your body. It can bring a smile to your face and lighten some of your sadness. This has happened to me when I recalled fond memories of Wishbone, and I caught myself smiling and feeling deep happiness for all that we shared. Writing this letter will give you the opportunity to be grateful for the time you had with your pet.

"Nothing that grieves us can be called little: by the eternal laws of proportion a child's loss of a doll and a king's loss of a crown are events of the same size."

—MARK TWAIN

Chapter 6

Understanding Types of Grief, Part 1: Anticipatory Grief

f your pet has been battling cancer or some other chronic disorder, or has been declining for some time, you most likely have been experiencing anticipatory grief. You may also experience it if your pet is elderly or if there is some other reason in the near future, such as a pending military deployment, that may cause you to lose your pet, either temporarily or permanently.

This chapter contains some material that is specific to anticipatory grief, including planning, pet hospice, and euthanasia.

You may also experience multiple types of loss, either at the same time or sequentially. As you know from my introduction where you met Wishbone, I experienced both anticipatory and ambiguous grief from his mental decline. It was ambiguous because I had already lost part of him, despite the fact that he was still physically with me. For complete information on ambiguous grief, see Chapter 7.

At the heart of the matter is the pain you are experiencing, regardless of the type of grief. Any type of grief can manifest as normal grief responses, which can include sadness, anger, guilt, and numbness.

ANTICIPATORY GRIEF

Most people think of grief as something that happens after a death. However, grieving can also occur before death, and this is known as anticipatory grief. It occurs as the result of the anticipation of a death or other type of loss. We can already be experiencing the loss of some of our pet's abilities due to the aging process. It may show up in your pet's lessened ability to walk and get around, a loss of appetite, or developing lethargy. We can be filled with overwhelming anxiety as our beloved pet slowly declines, and we experience a slow or accelerating loss of our pet's quality of life.

We can also experience anticipatory grief if we receive news that our pet has a terminal illness and that death will most certainly follow.

As sad and difficult as this grief is, it may be helpful for you in some ways, as it provides you with some warning of your pet's impending death and allows you time to prepare.

Anticipatory grief can certainly carry many of the same symptoms as acute grief (described in Chapter 7). You may find yourself experiencing anger, guilt, sadness, a lack of concentration, and even depression. Anticipatory grief can also manifest itself in feelings of fatigue and exhaustion from intense caring for your pet and coping with the reality of their impending death.

REACHING OUT IS ESSENTIAL TO YOUR HEALING

Since this type of grief can be combined with exhaustion from being an intense caregiver for your pet, it is essential that you take care of yourself and stay connected to caring family and friends. No doubt, this is a very challenging time for you.

A Time to Embrace Your Pet's Death; A Time for Acceptance

Anticipatory grief begins when you either suddenly or slowly start to see the signs of a decline in your pet, and you decide to consult a vet with your concerns. Then the unbearable happens. Your mind races and questions accumulate. Quietly, the reality sinks in; your pet's life will not be as long as you had hoped for. Your pet may be in pain or, in my Wishbone's case, losing cognitive function. After some time, and with an inner struggle and turmoil, you decide that, despite your resistance, you need to accept what is going to happen. You begin grieving for what has already become an unbearable loss, the loss of the pet whom you knew for all these years. Despite the changes that are occurring, your love will always remain to give you strength during these difficult challenges.

The reality of what is occurring can help you prepare for life without your cherished pet. It can offer you the opportunity to spend more quality time with your pet, and it can help you to begin to embrace the approaching death and plan your pet's final days. You may experience some hope at first that the situation can turn itself around, only to later divert your energy away from hope for recovery and begin to acknowledge the inevitable.

Some people create bucket lists for their pets as they face their impending death and deal with the roller coaster of emotions. All these final acts of love can enhance your pet's final days and allow you more memorable time with them. Of course, you can do something like taking your pet to their favorite walking or play areas, or giving them their special treats a little more frequently if their circumstances allow for it. Doing something extra special for your pet may help ease the pain of their approaching death for you. The most important thing you can do is spend that very special time with them, talking with them, telling them how important they have been in your life, cuddling with them, and telling them of your love for them. I believe you both will find some comfort. You can prepare some of their favorite food treats if you think they can tolerate them. I know Wishbone loved sweet potatoes as well as peanut butter, and both were included in his final days.

As hard as it is as you focus on the continued care and support for your cherished pet, it is vital to remember to take care of yourself. Book some time in your calendar for self-care and take this appointment seriously, to ease your stress and renew your energy. Everyone involved will react and cope differently with this approaching loss, and that is okay. What's important here is what you can do to control this situation. Keeping the lines of communication open and including everyone in the important decisions are essential for all concerned. It's also important to keep others who care about you informed, because you don't have to go through this alone.

Many questions and concerns will arise when you receive a life-threatening diagnosis or are dealing with age-related issues that result in a lower quality of life for your pet. You will have things to ask your vet and the other significant people in your life. Take some deep breaths and a few minutes to assess the situation. Expect to have some turmoil in your life, but keep in mind there are others who want to help you through this, so please reach out.

You are wise to learn all you can about your pet's diagnosis and possible treatment options, including getting a second opinion. Your finances will also need to be taken into account. While it is extremely difficult to think about your pet's final months, days, or even moments, it is important to begin to make some decisions about their future. As you continue to accept the reality of your pet's impending death, it may be helpful for you to list some possible questions for your subsequent visits to your vet's office. Obviously, your questions will vary depending on your situation, but here is a good basic list with which to start:

- Does this diagnosis mean that my pet will experience a lot of pain?

- Are there any types of medications that can be given to my pet to help with their pain?

- How about other treatments that can help my pet be more comfortable, such as chiropractic, massage, water therapy, or acupuncture services?

- Do you have a time frame of how long my pet's remaining life might be?

- What about hospice care for my pet? Can my pet die peacefully at home? (More on hospice care below.)

- Do I need to think about euthanasia? When? (More on euthanasia below.)

As difficult as an anticipatory loss is, it provides a window of opportunity to allow you to begin to grieve and plan for your pet's passing.

As you go through this very challenging time in anticipation of your pet's death, please keep in mind that experiencing anticipatory grief will neither speed up nor slow down your grief after your pet's death. Unfortunately, in some respects, it is almost like a double death that you have to endure.

What about Hospice Care for My Pet?

Veterinary hospice is for dogs and cats (Lap of Love Veterinary Hospice & In-Home Euthanasia 2022) and is a team-oriented service that helps to maintain the quality and comfort of their remaining life until natural death occurs. Pet hospice was originally modeled after human hospice. If your pet has a terminal illness, or if you are managing advanced aging in your pet, hospice is something to consider. This type of care is focused on the comfort of your pet during the time leading up to their death. It is not about finding a cure for whatever they are dealing with. Depending on your pet's condition, you may be able to keep him or her comfortable in your own home with support from your veterinarian and your family or friends. Everyone's situation is different, as each pet has varying amounts of pain and other circumstances that need to be considered. Consult with your veterinarian if you are interested in hospice for your pet. He or she can help you determine if it is something that will be helpful at this stage of their illness. Lap of Love (https://www.lapoflove.com/) is a nationwide hospice program, and there may be a member veterinarian in your locality. They also have a helpful "Quality-of-Life Scale" you can use to evaluate your pet. There may be other similar organizations in your area. It is important to gather information about possible choices you may have open to you in dealing with your pet's health. An informed decision will give you the peace of mind you deserve and comfort for your pet at the end of their life.

Do I Need to Consider Euthanasia?

Depending on what your pet is going through, you may need to consider euthanasia.

The word "euthanasia" is derived from two Greek words, "eu" meaning "good" and "thanatos" meaning "death." These words would then describe euthanasia as a "good death." "Loving" and "humane" are two words associated with euthanasia (Lagoni, Butler, and Hetts 1994).

Euthanasia is a decision that can be made with your vet and should include the people in your circle who have a bond with your pet. It requires careful thought and discussion with others who care. The following are some things to consider:

🐾 What is the current activity level of your pet? Does your pet still enjoy activities that they previously enjoyed, or have they already reached a level of relative inactivity?

🐾 Does your pet still interact with and respond to others in their life, or do they seem confused or disoriented?

🐾 Are you aware if they are experiencing pain and suffering that take away from their enjoyment of life?

🐾 Is your pet facing certain death from an injury or terminal illness?

🐾 Is everyone involved in your pet's care comfortable with a decision to euthanize, or is someone hesitant? Can everyone live with the decision they voice their opinion on?

I can echo many of my past clients' voices when I share that, even when the decision is medically necessary and a beloved pet is clearly suffering, it is still one of the hardest decisions to make. It is gut wrenching. If you choose euthanasia for your pet, you may experience many thoughts that nag at your very core. You may wonder whether, if you had chosen a different treatment plan, they might still be here. If your pet was in an accident that led to the decision to choose euthanasia, you may blame yourself instead of the real cause for your choice—the accident. You may feel guilty because you didn't spend more quality time with your pet before their passing. The important thing here is to feel confident you are making a decision in the best interest of your beloved pet, regardless of whether you seek further treatments, choose hospice, or choose euthanasia. Consult with people whom you trust, and do some of your own research, especially if this isn't a decision that needs to be made immediately. Gather all the information you can by talking with a trusted vet and perhaps getting a second opinion.

If you decide to have your pet euthanized, here are a few

things for you and your loved ones to consider before the procedure. It may be helpful for you to have a special notebook to write down any additional questions you may have and to record some of the information that is relayed back to you. Of utmost importance is the fact that you want your pet to be treated with respect and compassion. This preplanning can be helpful before you actually need to make this major decision for your pet. It will allow you to gather your thoughts and information for decisions for the welfare of your pet. You will be able to think more clearly because you are not in the middle of a crisis. If your pet has major injuries and euthanasia is more imminent, the advance planning will still be helpful, as you most likely will be in a better position to understand what will be unfolding in a more immediate way.

1. Does my vet offer euthanasia to my pet in my home or other non-office space?

Your vet may offer the option of in-home euthanasia. Everyone has different preferences; discuss yours with your vet. If you prefer in-home euthanasia and your vet doesn't offer it, prepare to research other vets in your area who might. If the procedure can be done at home, it can be more calming and reassuring for your pet and other family members, including other family pets. Everyone can be together for support, and the family pets will also be able to witness and readily sniff their furry housemate after the death. This allows them to say goodbye in their own way. On the other hand, the vet's office may be a familiar place that doesn't make them anxious. There is no right or wrong way here; take time to think about what the two scenarios will look and feel like, and make the decision based on what is best for all involved.

2. What typically occurs during euthanasia?

Discuss this question with your vet and anyone else involved in a close relationship with your pet. You may also want to confer with a trusted friend who has experienced this procedure with their pets. Keep in mind, each person's experience will vary. This topic is explored in the next two paragraphs, but a full discussion with your own vet is very important, as their individual office procedures can vary from this information.

3. Is it always a two-step injection, the first being a sedative and the second the final one that brings death?

This is something to discuss with the vet and express your concerns. The injection of the sedative will cause your pet to become very drowsy. You may have a window of time to spend with your pet as they continue to go into a deeper sleep. Hold your pet in your arms as you talk to them, and tell them how much you love them and that they will always live on in your heart. Personally, I believe they will know you are there until their last breath. Maybe you would like to sing quietly to your pet, or very gently cradle them, if possible. They may still have some level of awareness, so continue to be calm and gentle. These are your last few moments alone as you say goodbye. The vet may return soon and administer the final injection. You can then spend more time with your beloved pet after their death. This might be a good time for other family pets who are waiting in the car or waiting room to come in for their goodbyes. It's actually good if they sniff their deceased family member. Make it known ahead of time if you are planning to take your beloved pet with you to bury or if you have chosen cremation. Bring a blanket to gently wrap your pet with dignity if you are bringing them home for burial or to a pet cemetery. Have all of your wishes written down so they can be followed. You have been through a heart-wrenching experience with your pet and helped to provide a peaceful death and an end to their suffering. You may feel like you had the wind knocked out of you, and ache in every fiber of your being. Use some of the breathing exercises in Chapter 9. Take time to care for yourself, and allow others to care for you. Be gentle with yourself. You have given your cherished pet a gift of love and freedom from pain. Focus on this now. Accept the love and hugs from family and friends. Your beloved pet is out of pain and lives on in your heart.

Will my pet be in pain? How long before death occurs? The first injection that your pet receives is a sedative that will allow them to become relaxed, drowsy, or unconscious. The first injection will make the second injection, the actual euthanasia drug, easier for the veterinarian. With the second injection, your beloved pet will become completely unconscious within a few seconds, and death will follow quickly. Your pet should not experience any pain through this subtle transition. Again, discuss any concerns or questions with your veterinarian.

4. Can I bring my pet home after their death so other family pets can see, touch, and smell their furry companion or playmate?

Ask if other family pets that had a relationship with your pet can be brought into the room to say their goodbye. A trusted friend or another person may be willing to care for the other pet or pets in the car and wait for the word to enter the clinic. Pets that have shared their lives together generally have a deep bond, and animals really do grieve the loss of a close furry companion.

5. After my beloved pet passes, do I want to have their body prepared for viewing at a funeral establishment? Do I want to hold a gathering of family and friends to honor my pet at the funeral establishment or at my home?

   Gather your thoughts, reflect, discuss them with others involved closely with your pet, and then write your decisions in your notebook. As the reality unfolds and your thinking gets cloudy, you will have the information at your disposal to refer to.

6. Do I want to have my pet buried in my backyard (if this is allowed in my community), or do I want my pet buried in a pet cemetery?

   If burial in your backyard is your choice, you need to check your local community for any restrictions. You also need to consider that this might not be a good option if you may be moving to another residence at some point.

   If cremation is your choice, you can choose individual or communal cremation, where multiple pets are cremated together. Do you want to purchase an urn or other container that you can keep in your home or have buried? If you like, you can also purchase jewelry online that will hold some of your pet's remains.

   The cost involved in any of the above choices will also need to be considered.

7. Let others who care about you and your pet know your plans.

   It will allow them to spend some time with your pet to say their final goodbyes, and it also alerts your caring community that you will need extra comforting in the coming days.

When talking about the process of euthanasia, it is important to use the correct words, as hard as it is. You are not "putting your pet to sleep" or "putting them down." This is very important when preparing family members for the eventual death of a family pet. As painful as it is to say and hear, children need to understand in a very loving way that the pet they have is not going to sleep and will not awaken the next day. Their spirit has left their body, and now we can always keep them alive within us with all of our memories. You are choosing a procedure that will eliminate life and pain in a very short time. You have provided a final gift of love to your cherished pet. You may wish to honor your pet's memory when you return home, and light a candle in their memory. It's a small way to soothe you through the initial phase of your pet's death.

In Chapter 11 you can read all the wonderful ways you can honor your pet's memory. Reflect on your time together and cherish all the time you had together, knowing you made the right decision. Above all else, keep in mind that choosing euthanasia is a very emotional decision. The loss of your pet can be devastating. They provided companionship, joy, laughter, and pure, unconditional love. You can grieve and begin the healing process, knowing you made the best decision for your pet if you chose a humane death from euthanasia. It may be helpful to keep a journal of your feelings and thoughts about your decision. You may wish to include your pet's symptoms and quality-of-life issues that prompted you to choose euthanasia. Writing about this process can help you clearly see that you made the best choice for your beloved family member. It may help to share this with a trusted friend, family member, or trained counselor who specializes in grief and loss. The memories we made with our pets will remain safely in our hearts, and talking about them will keep their memories alive.

I wish you peace, comfort, and continued healing.

REFLECTIVE WRITING
EXPERIENCES

CHAPTER 6:

Understanding Types of Grief, Part 1: Anticipatory Grief Writing Experience—Exploring Your Grief, Part 1

Anticipatory grief frequently feels the same as grief from an actual physical loss. It can become complicated because you now have the knowledge of your pet's impending departure. Validate feelings by expressing them in the form of writing. It will be helpful to reflect on what you wrote. It will help you to better understand and express your feelings to caring people. It can also be beneficial to plan for this stage of your pet's life.

Please continue on to the second reflective exercise when you feel ready, and write out some of the questions that you can address by yourself or with your vet, family, and trusted friends. After completing these exercises, you may want to check Chapter 9 (Taking Care of You) and follow some of the suggestions to help you through this very difficult time.

Writing Experience—Exploring Your Grief, Part 2

Consider how you would like to spend the remaining time you have together with your pet. Enhancing your pet's life as you go through this stage can include having a comfortable space for them to rest and spending additional quality time with them.

Check out the reference in Appendix B for a bucket list for pets. Write down questions for your vet, such as "How much time?" "Are they in pain now?" and "How do I know when it may be time to make the final decision?"

Advance planning for your pet's impending death can help alleviate some of your anxiety and allow you to focus on providing your pet with continued compassionate care. Your grieving heart can be eased by making their final days more meaningful with their favorite toys and snacks, but most importantly with your continued love and support.

"Death ends a life, not a relationship."

—JACK LEMMON

Chapter 7

Understanding Types of Grief, Part 2: Acute, Ambiguous, Disenfranchised, and Complicated Grief

his chapter highlights and focuses on names and descriptions of grief that you may have already experienced in your loss or you may experience later. It is important to understand this information so that you gain the knowledge to help now in your grief journey and are prepared for what may lie ahead. Grief comes in many faces and disguises, and you may experience different types of grief as part of your grief journey. Knowledge is power, and that knowledge helps to bring us to a clearer understanding of what may be in your path.

There are common factors in all types of grief. They all result from a loss. The different types of grief include the following (Karaban 2000):

- ❧ Acute grief
- ❧ Anticipatory grief (already covered separately in Chapter 6)
- ❧ Ambiguous grief
- ❧ Disenfranchised grief
- ❧ Complicated grief (also called "prolonged grief")

You may experience multiple types of loss at the same time or sequentially. As you know from my introduction, where you met Wishbone, I experienced anticipatory and ambiguous grief from his mental decline. Skippy was my aunt's dog when I was a very young child. I was very fond of him, and whenever we went to visit, I enjoyed playing with him. One day when I went to visit, he was gone, and I never found out what happened to him. My loss was both ambiguous and disenfranchised. I recently received an old photograph of him with me, and it triggered feelings of sadness once again, but also the happy memory of him in my heart.

These questions, and ones like them, are helpful to determine what kind of loss or grief you are experiencing. Once you determine that, you will be better equipped to discuss your loss with somebody else and to understand it better yourself: Was your pet involved in an accident? Was your pet severely injured? Or did your pet die tragically and suddenly? Maybe there is a custody battle that involves your pet? Are you dealing with the real possibility that you may not have custody of your pet? Are you anticipating that you might never see your pet again? So many thoughts, questions, and concerns may weigh heavily on you.

At the heart of the matter is the pain you are experiencing, regardless of the type of grief. Any type of grief can manifest as normal grief responses; these include sadness, anger, guilt, and numbness.

THE EMOTION OF GRIEF

Grief can include a broad range of feelings, such as sadness, emptiness, anger, and guilt. Grief can also include transient physical complaints, such as sleeping and eating disturbances. Some or all of these feelings and behaviors are common as a normal response to grief, but what you experience is unique to you. You may or may not experience any or all of these reactions when you are on your grief journey, and that is why grief is unique to each and every individual.

Working through your grief can be physically and emotionally draining. There are healthy ways to deal with the grief you are experiencing, such as expressing your grief in words to others that are in your life and care about you and who want to support you during this difficult time. Unhealthy ways of expressing grief can manifest in overeating, sleeping excessively, not connecting to others, and generally not attending to your physical body. Unhealthy ways to cope don't help you and can cause you to get stuck and not manage your feelings. The healthy ways of coping with your feelings alleviate some of your pain and help you continue to express your feelings.

The intensity or duration of your grief may change and affect your ability to function in your daily life, such as by causing difficulty getting up for the day and attending to your physical needs. If that happens, then it is time to consider bringing it to the attention of a medical doctor or a trained grief and loss counselor. The intensity or duration of your grief may be a signal of complicated grief. It can manifest in uncontrollable feelings and thoughts that interfere with your ability to function in your daily life.

ACUTE GRIEF

Acute grief is the grief you typically feel immediately after a loss or the death of a loved one. It is sometimes referred to as "normal grief," but, personally, I do not agree with that term, because it incorrectly implies that one specific manifestation of grief is "normal" and all others are "abnormal." Remember, *everyone's grief is unique.*

Grief has been described as a psychological syndrome that includes intense physical, emotional, and behavioral symptoms.

Acute grief either passes or becomes complicated grief (described later in this chapter). Here are many of the ways in which acute grief manifests itself:

- Body pains
- Sighing frequently
- Empty feeling in stomach
- Shortness of breath
- Tightness in throat
- Muscle weakness
- Sleeplessness that can lead to fatigue
- Palpitations
- Nausea
- Crying
- Feelings of disbelief
- Feelings of guilt, sadness, fear, loneliness
- Apathy
- Anxiety
- Panic
- Feelings of emptiness
- Numbness
- Isolating from others
- Restlessness
- Absentmindedness
- Difficulty concentrating
- Trouble keeping up with normal daily activities
- Thinking about your own death
- Obsessing about the loved one's death

This is not an exhaustive list, but it does include the most commonly recognized ways of experiencing grief.

AMBIGUOUS LOSS AND GRIEF:
A GRIEF WITH MUCH UNCERTAINTY

Ambiguous loss has confusion or a lack of clarity surrounding the loss itself. There is a lack of certainty regarding either the loss itself or when the uncertainty will end (Karaban 2000). One example of this type of loss is a beloved pet who is physically alive but has a condition that makes him or her unavailable emotionally. Another example is a pet who is physically alive but no longer present because of dementia or some other debilitating condition. This was the case with my dog Wishbone, whom you met in the introduction to this book.

Wishbone was a vital part of our family's life. We had a deep bond with him, and he impacted our lives in many ways, most importantly providing us with pure unconditional love. He was quick to gently hop on our laps whenever he sensed a need for a special cuddle, and always ready to bring laughter to us with his silly antics and playful manner. Wishbone was also quick to alert us to any sign of potential trouble.

It was emotionally draining to see Wishbone change from a vibrant family member into an emotionally aloof dog who was unfamiliar to us. The lack of the meaningful ways in which he had contributed to our lives was unsettling. We longed for the parts of Wishbone that were now hidden, even though we were glad he was still with us. Our tears flowed, and the loss of the structure he provided for our lives was at times very noticeable. For me, it led to procrastination in getting some things accomplished. It showed as an emptiness and gut-wrenching pain in the very fabric of my being, and it produced various body aches. How I longed for the real Wishbone!

Time elapsed, and the void became deeper. We felt a need to interact with another dog in the ways that we no longer could with Wishbone. We also thought another dog might help Wishbone with his memory issues and with being alone when we were at work. At first, we thought we should wait until after Wishbone passed, but an opportunity arose where another Jack Russell terrier needed a new home. We set up a meeting with the six-month-old puppy, and it was "love at first sight." Jazzy became the newest member of our family. We wish she could have had more contact with Wishbone before he passed, as he was sure to have been a great teacher. Having Jazzy before Wishbone died certainly helped me in dealing with Wishbone's death. She did not replace Wishbone, of course, as he was a dynamic dog with his own individual personality. It was beneficial to know we were caring for and loving another dog that needed a forever home. Having Jazzy allowed us to continue to mourn Wishbone and to celebrate his life as well as to be grateful for having the opportunity to make a difference in another animal's life.

Wishbone was physically present, but mentally absent. Hence, our loss and grief were ambiguous until he passed. Ambiguous loss and grief also includes situations in which a pet might be physically missing, and you do not know if you will ever see them again. This can be through something like a natural disaster, or your pet leaving the yard and getting lost or even stolen.

You are probably experiencing ambiguous loss when you have questions like these: Where is my pet? What happened? What caused their death? Will I ever see them again? What a very sad time not having any answers to these questions, not having closure! The uncertainty is overwhelming. Guilt, anger, and sadness may permeate your entire being.

Losing a pet this way paves the way for so much uncertainty. We have all seen signs posted with "Lost Pet" on them. Sometimes they are found and returned joyfully to their human families. Sometimes they find their own way home. And, sometimes, they are never seen again.

Ambiguous loss can happen either individually or on a massive scale from a natural disaster. For an example of a massive scale, after the devastating Hurricane Katrina, many pets were separated and lost from their families. However, there was good cause for not losing hope. Over the years, many rescue operations have found, saved, and cared for many pets that have either been adopted out or reunited with their families, even after several years. Stories abound about the unselfish work done on behalf of our beloved pets. We have heard stories about people being rescued and being in agony over not being able to take their pets with them. We have also heard stories of many animals rescued and reunited with their families. An important message here is "Never lose hope."

Here's one of the stories with a happy ending. William Morgan was rescued from the rising waters of Hurricane Katrina and was forced to abandon his dog, Miss Morgan. He was sped away in a boat, eventually ending up in a Veterans Affairs hospital in Miami. He sadly remembered Miss Morgan whimpering on the rooftop of his home; he'd still been able to hear her from several blocks away as the boat continued to bring him to safety. Fortunately, volunteers from the Best Friends Animal Society rescued her, along with thousands of other pets, after she'd spent twelve days alone on the rooftop. They placed her in an emergency shelter. More volunteers spent endless hours checking rescue information websites and found Miss Morgan. A few weeks later, Animal Planet covered a very happy reunion of Mr. Morgan and Miss Morgan at the VA hospital (Grimm 2015). This is a wonderful story of love and luck, for both Mr. Morgan and his dog, Miss Morgan. I can visualize what a happy reunion this must have been for Mr. Morgan!

Ambiguous loss causes so many unanswered questions, confusion, and even isolation, as we can encounter situations where there is little to no closure around the loss of our beloved pets. Ambiguous grief, or grief that is unresolved, can take over our lives. There is, unfortunately, the very real possibility that an episode of ambiguous grief may never be satisfactorily resolved or even fully recognized by others. While many of these losses may eventually have a resolution, others never will. This makes an ambiguous loss especially difficult to process.

DISENFRANCHISED GRIEF

Perhaps you can identify with a disenfranchised loss. This is a loss that others may not consider to be a "true loss." It is the kind of loss that does not get as much sympathy, care, or attention from others as would the death of a human family member. In disenfranchised grief, the expressions of sympathy and understanding are missing; the cards, memorials, and casseroles are not forthcoming. Disenfranchised grief, sometimes called "hidden grief," is from a loss that is not openly acknowledged or is socially minimized. This is very common for pet loss, and it can cause someone to mourn alone without any support. It makes you feel that you have to constantly explain to others that your pet was truly a family member and that this loss really hurts. Those problematic responses—such as "It was only a dog/cat" or "You can get another one"—come from people who don't really mean any harm, but rather have a hard time understanding grief over a pet. Many are very uncomfortable with grief in general and may not have had much experience in dealing with grief, be it their own or someone else's.

The support one commonly receives after a family member or good friend dies is generally absent when a beloved pet dies. They are our family too, but their death is often devalued. It's possible that others in your life really do want to help but are feeling inadequate with expressions and words. Another thing to consider is that many people may have never had a close relationship with an animal. Sometimes people really do care but just have a difficult time dealing with the emotional needs of another. So we do what we can to show them understanding, and one day they may be able to understand the unique loss of a pet, and perhaps validate that loss to a grieving person.

In our culture it is not easy to grieve and say goodbye, especially in the case of the loss of our pets. Not only do individuals often not understand, but social norms do not recognize the concept of grief at the loss of a pet. This loss is socially minimized, and instead of being given family bereavement time, we may feel we are forced to suppress and hide our sorrow. When was the last time you remember an employer giving someone time off for the loss of their pet? Time away can be an opportunity to reorganize your home surroundings and aid you in adjusting to daily life without your beloved pet. If you are employed and have personal time or family leave time, consider using it. Clients have shared with me that when the grief was unbearable, they would use sick time from work. They felt they might be teased about being absent from work over the death of their pet or otherwise not have their grief validated.

Disenfranchised grief can cause someone to feel a sense of shame when they express their grief, and may also expose them to many hurtful statements. Because of this, they may be reluctant to fully mourn their loss. Such statements and the failure of family or friends to recognize the relationship and deep connection between a person and their pet cause disenfranchised grief to continue. One can question, "Maybe I am overreacting to this loss?" A loss of a pet is absolutely a legitimate loss, and it needs to be grieved. Please don't let others devalue your loss. Losses that are not mourned can resurface later, sometimes triggered by another loss. That, in turn, can result in an uncontrollable cascade of emotions (deep sadness, guilt, and anger) rising to the surface. Unresolved grief can raise havoc in all parts of our lives. It's important to attend to our grief, mourn our loss, and address how our life will look without our pet.

When we return to the emptiness of our home at the end of

our workday with no physical presence of our beloved pet, we clearly miss the warm welcome from our pet. One client shared with me that after the euthanasia of her pet, she was so grief-stricken that she could not return to the home she had shared with her pet. She felt she needed to retreat to a hotel room, to rest and reflect on how she would begin the slow adjustment to life without her beloved dog. Perhaps time away is something that might be helpful to you. It would be a time to reflect on all that has happened and to begin to prepare yourself to return to the home that you shared with your pet. Take it slowly and give yourself a gift of time. As we all grieve differently, we also find comfort differently.

COMPLICATED GRIEF

Complicated grief is characterized by its intensity and duration. It can manifest in uncontrollable feelings and thoughts that interfere with a person's ability to function in their daily lives. These thoughts, feelings, and behaviors may continue for long periods of time, and no change or improvement seems to follow. Most of the time, people who have complicated grief have had an unusually close and rewarding relationship with their pet. Our loving pets give us so much and ask for so little. Their unconditional, non-judgmental love is uncomplicated and helps to bring some stability to our daily lives. Clearly, their deaths have a tremendous impact on us.

Many of the symptoms of complicated grief are the same as symptoms of acute grief. However, they are typically more intense or more extreme and may go on much longer. The following can be signs of complicated grief.

- The sorrow is intense, and the pain never seems to end.

- Obsessive thoughts are present in your daily life.

- There is a lack of acceptance of the death.

- You long achingly for the person or pet you lost.

- You experience a feeling of numbness.

- You feel you cannot trust others.

- You don't enjoy life anymore.

- Life seems to have no purpose.

- Your ability to engage in necessary daily activities is very limited.

- You isolate yourself from others.

- Sadness becomes your worldview.

- You have become stuck in sadness and depression.

- You find yourself thinking obsessively about your pet's death and your own death.

This type of grief generally does not resolve without professional assistance. You may need to seek help from a qualified therapist. There is no shame in reaching out for help; on the contrary, it is much to your credit. Individual therapy, support groups, and support phone lines are available. Information on support lines is included in Appendix B at the end of this book. You don't have to journey through this alone. Reaching out for help can allow you to address your concerns from your loss and to receive validation, support, and a course of action to address your grief. Be gentle with yourself, and give yourself the gift of the same loving care you gave to your beloved pet.

TRIGGERS FOR GRIEF

As you continue on your grief journey, it is important to be aware of some potential triggers for your grief. Triggers are reminders of your loss that may open you up to a range of feelings that can stop you in your tracks. They can happen at any time and can bring on great sadness and longing for your pet. Potential triggers include the following:

- A particular place that had special meaning for you and your pet
- A special date that was celebrated
- An object that belonged to your pet
- Seeing another pet that reminds you of your pet that died
- First anniversaries

Some triggers can be obvious, but some may sneak up on you and surprise you in unexpected ways. Triggers can be unpredictable, but planning for the obvious ones can help you. For example, if you know that the anniversary of your pet's passing may raise your anxiety, then plan on being around loved ones whom you trust and who understand what you have experienced. It's important to be prepared for the potential reaction from this trigger. Try to stay focused on all the wonderful memories you made with your cherished pet, and plan a special activity to continue to honor and celebrate their life with you.

First anniversaries can be opportunities for fresh insights. You may experience grief that awakens more vigorously as you anticipate the "first anniversaries." These might be the first holidays at which your beloved pet is not present, an anniversary of their birthday, the anniversary of their death, or any special first anniversary you may encounter. You can reflect on these "firsts" and allow yourself that cry that you still need. It is okay! Maybe you can start a new "memory tradition" by celebrating, commemorating, and honoring the life and love of your dear pet and all the contributions they made to your life. Maybe at that time you can plan a celebration party. Remember as well, they were most fortunate to have you in their life. You can also check out the many other ideas for remembering your pet in Chapter 11 (Remembering and Honoring Your Pet).

Keep in mind that your grief can ebb and flow, and triggers may continue to come up that can activate your grief response and make you feel that it is unbearable. When the grief is flowing, engage in some helping activities to soothe yourself. Now you have more knowledge and know it is very important that you continue to express your feelings to those who care. Grief takes time; be patient with yourself. Accept that this loss has changed your life, and know that the reality is that you may never completely get over the death of your pet. You will move forward without the physical presence of your pet. Your pain will soften, and the intensity of your grief will lessen. There is hope for your future without your cherished pet that has died. Embrace the new reality, and know that others care for you. Stay connected to life.

I wish you peace, comfort, and continued healing.

REFLECTIVE WRITING
EXPERIENCES

CHAPTER 7:

Understanding Types of Grief, Part 2: Acute, Ambiguous,
Disenfranchised, and Complicated Grief
Writing Experience—Exploring Your Grief

Do you feel you are experiencing any of these particular types of grief—acute, ambiguous, disenfranchised, or complicated? If so, it would be helpful to write about what you are feeling so that you can reflect on and better understand it. If you are experiencing any physical sensations, please elaborate on them in your writing. Be sure to include any specific thoughts or feelings that you are experiencing, such as sadness, anger, frustration, and so forth. Your writing can help you to clarify what you are feeling and experiencing.

"When you are sorrowful look again in your heart,
and you shall see that in truth you are weeping for that
which has been your delight."

— KHALIL GIBRAN

Chapter 8

Using Tools to Organize Your Thoughts and Feelings

nformation about any type of grief or loss generally includes a mention of the work of Swiss psychiatrist Elisabeth Kübler-Ross (McVean 2019) and psychologist J. William Worden (Worden 2009). I am including a summary of the former's model and the latter's framework, in case you find one or both of them helpful. Each has a model or framework that has been extensively used for grief work and that can help you organize your thoughts and feelings. You will then be better able to share them with others and reflect on them yourself.

GRIEF HAS A WAY OF EBBING AND FLOWING

Your grief belongs to you alone. The experiences you are going through can be intense at times, and their duration is unknown. Some days it feels like this process is over, and then at some later time, you can feel like you've been hit by a sudden windstorm. A memory of your pet can come out of the blue and trigger intense feelings. The important thing is to recognize above all else that your feelings are normal and are specific to you. Please don't compare your feelings to another's. We all grieve differently.

THE NOT-REALLY-STAGES BY PSYCHIATRIST ELISABETH KÜBLER-ROSS

Let's cover Elisabeth Kübler-Ross first, as her work is more widely known. She developed what many refer to as five stages that one may go through in dealing with grief and loss issues (McVean 2019).

However, instead of being a model for the stages of grief, it is actually a model for people with life-threatening illnesses, and it characterizes their adjustment to the diagnosis of a terminal illness. Not everyone goes through all of them or goes in a prescribed order. As Dr. Kübler-Ross herself explicitly stated in a later book, "The five stages are not some stops on a linear timeline in grief. They cannot be universal, because every culture and every person grieves differently. Assuming that they are universal only causes more pain."

I present this information as something that may be helpful for you. However, I consider the stages to really be tools to help us identify and organize what we may be feeling. The five stages in the Kübler-Ross model are Denial, Anger, Bargaining, Depression, and Acceptance. Since they are not events that happen in some particular order, I refer to them as "reactions." For clarity, I will keep Kübler-Ross's terms.

The Reactions

Using Kübler-Ross's stages, I have expanded on how they are potential *reactions* you might encounter as you grieve the loss of your pet. They are some thoughts or emotions you may experience. Please keep in mind and continue to reflect that not everyone may relate to this particular list. You may not experience all of them or experience them in any particular order. This is normal. Honor who you are!

Remember, the key here is: *Everyone experiences their grief in a very individual, unique, personal way and in no particular order or timeframe.* Here are the reactions you *may* have:

1. **Reactions of Denial:** This may manifest as feelings of numbness, shock, and dismay. You can't wrap your head around this. *Did my beautiful cherished pet really die? How can this be happening?*

2. **Reactions of Anger:** You may be angry at the vet who cared for your pet, angry at yourself for not being near when your pet died, and even angry at others because they are not grieving like you are. *I can't believe this is really happening to me. I can't believe it! Why doesn't anybody understand why I am hurting so much? My pet was my best friend.*

3. **Reactions of Bargaining:** *Okay, maybe we can make a deal.* You may try to make a bargain with a higher power if your pet is ill: *I will do this if my pet gets better.* This may be a time when you think of a lot of "if onlys" and "what ifs": *If only we'd taken our pet to the vet sooner. If only we'd had that surgery or test for our pet. What if I'd gone to a different vet who is a specialist?*

4. **Reactions of Depression:** You may feel overwhelming sadness and emptiness. It may be difficult to go about your daily activities. You may experience poor appetite, sleep disturbances, difficulty concentrating, or frequent sadness. These are normal reactions to a loss.

5. **Reactions of Acceptance:** After some time, you will begin to feel that things will be okay. You may never stop missing your beloved pet, but you feel ready to move on. Moving on does not mean you will ever forget your pet or the special relationship you had together. Moving on means your pet will live on forever in your heart. You can accept

now that your life will never be the same. Moving on may also mean you can once again share your life with another pet. Another pet will not ever replace the beloved pet that you lost. Instead, you may bring another pet into your life and love them for their own special personality, and for the unique love and relationship that you will have with them.

FRAMEWORK BY PSYCHOLOGIST J. WILLIAM WORDEN

Another framework for grief work is by psychologist J. William Worden (Worden 2009). His framework includes four tasks that can help us understand how we might journey through grief. He notes that healing happens gradually as grievers address these tasks, in no specific order, going back and forth from one to another over time. This information will help you organize your thoughts and feelings. It will also raise your level of awareness to a more comprehensive understanding of grief and the things that can help move you along in this journey.

I have added my thoughts on Worden's "tasks" to help you relate to them specifically over the loss of your pet.

Task 1: To Accept the Reality of the Loss

Although you know intellectually that your pet has died, you may experience a sense of disbelief. Integrating the reality of their death means "taking it in" with your whole being. For example, the reality may begin to set in immediately after the death, when you realize that your pet is no longer in your home.

Many weeks, months, or years later when an occasion arises that they would have been part of, the reality again hits you as you realize that your pet has died and isn't here to share these moments with you.

The reality is your beloved pet has died, whether suddenly or expectedly because of declining health or progressive illness, and it surely is a difficult time. If this has been an anticipated death, perhaps you had time to set things in process for the burial or cremation. You know in your mind your pet has died, but your heart needs to catch up with your brain. The days leading up to when your pet died may have been exhausting for you, and sometimes our brain plays tricks on us. *Did my cherished pet really die or is this a bad dream? My pet has left this world!* The reality begins to sink in, and you are heartbroken.

The anniversary of the loss of your pet and the anniversary of the day your pet became a part of your life can trigger you to revisit the feelings of your loss and cause a deep emptiness. To ease your pain at these times, try making a gratitude list of all the wonderful memories you have of your pet. You can also plan a walk in a nature area and savor the beauty, listen to the birds, watch the squirrels running around, and check out the different trees, shrubs, and flowers.

Task 2: To Process the Pain of Grief

Grief can be experienced emotionally, cognitively, physically, behaviorally, and spiritually.

People may be telling you: "Get over it; move on; be strong." In contrast, one of the aims of grief support groups is to encourage and facilitate the safe expression of all the natural grief reactions.

Yes, grief can be felt in all areas of your being. It is important to address all the areas. Recognize the importance of keeping a balance in your life, with both daily exercise and time for rest. Keep up with your interests and develop new ones, reach out to others, and don't suppress your feelings. Take the time you need to grieve.

Task 3: To Adjust to a World without the Deceased

External adjustments include taking on new daily responsibilities and learning new skills.

Internal adjustments are made as you adapt to your new identity.

Spiritual adjustments occur as you grapple with questions about your belief system and the purpose and meaning of life.

Your beloved pet is no longer with you, and your life will never be the same. You never get used to it, but you somehow manage to move forward, knowing that there may be some difficult days ahead as you continue to mourn for your pet. In those trying days, engage with people and in things that help, and avoid people and things that don't help. It may be comforting to pull out your photos or memory book and focus on the gratitude you have for your pet having been in your life. And know that your pet would thank you for living their life with you.

Task 4: To Find an Enduring Connection with the Deceased in the Midst of Embarking on a New Life

Gradually you create a balance between remembering the pet who died and living a full and meaningful life (based on J. W. Worden [2009]).

The treasured memories of you and your pet will always be available to you, so make time for quiet in your life to savor those memories. Revisit the good times with them. Reflect and write about the time you welcomed your pet into your home and how you decided on their name. You can also describe their favorite toy. For help, you can check back on any of the writing activities you were able to do, and add more to them.

"Death leaves a heartache no one can heal, love leaves a memory no one can steal."

—IRISH HEADSTONE

THE LOSS HURTS

You have suffered a loss that hurts, and sometimes you just need to take life one moment at a time. It is vital that you be kind to yourself, and remember that this transition in your life can be life altering. It will be important during this grief process for you to follow some self-care rituals. The time to start doing them is now. What is most important is to find something that works for you, and do it on a consistent basis. It might be going for that walk in a nature area, creating that craft or sewing project, getting that massage, engaging with family and friends, or having some much-needed "me" time. Keep reaching out to trusted friends and family.

Keep in mind that your grief may awaken after a pause, and it can ebb and flow as time goes on. Times this may happen include the anniversary of the day your pet came into your life or the anniversary of your pet's death. When this happens, you can look over some of the suggestions in this book for things that might help you along in your grief journey. *You* are important and deserve to feel better.

REFLECTIVE WRITING
EXPERIENCES

CHAPTER 8:
Using Tools to Organize Your Thoughts and Feelings
Writing Experience—Grief Work

Psychiatrist Elisabeth Kübler-Ross's model and psychologist J. William Worden's framework for grief work presented in this chapter can help you organize your thoughts and feelings. What part of the information can you identify with specifically? What do you need to work on now?

For example, you may feel that Task 4 in Worden's framework ("To find an enduring connection with the deceased in the midst of embarking on a new life") is one you want to address in this writing activity. What are some of the things you would like to do to honor your pet's memory and can help to keep their memory alive, either now or in the future?

Write your thoughts on this, reflect on what you wrote, and then jot down any additional insights you may have gained from this exercise. Maybe you can then do one thing to honor the memory of your pet. Refer back to what you wrote at a later time and add any further thoughts or reflections.

"What we have once enjoyed we can never lose. All that we love deeply becomes a part of us."

—HELEN KELLER

SECTION III

Coping with Grief

The chapters in this third section give specific recommendations regarding how to take care of you and the people around you. They contain useful strategies and skills you can use now and in the future to cope with the flood of emotions and to bring some calm and relaxation to your life.

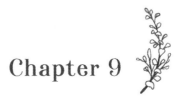

Chapter 9

Taking Care of You

ou are important, and attending to your grief by taking care of you is necessary for your healing. In this chapter, I share some of the most helpful things that you can do to take care of yourself while you move through your grief journey. The brief list includes some things that will definitely help you get started quickly on this important self-care. You can flip back to this chapter at different times to remind yourself to try something that you haven't tried before. Your reactions to your loss will change. What is helpful now might not be helpful later, and what does not help now might help in the future.

The loss of a pet causes a deep void in our lives. The emptiness can be overwhelming. Anyone who has had a bond with an animal knows how much our pet family member meant to us.

Please don't let anyone devalue or disenfranchise your loss by saying, "It's only a . . ." or telling you how to feel.

I believe your pet would want you to be good to yourself. Feel free to spend more time on the particular feelings of loss that are affecting you right now. If you are having strong feelings of sadness, anger, or frustration, give yourself permission to have a good cry or to punch a pillow. Grieving can zap your energy, cause you to feel numb, and adversely affect your concentration. These are common reactions in people who are grieving. It's okay to take that short nap or to curl up on the couch with a blanket and warm heat from a hot pack to nurture yourself. When you are feeling up to it, slowly begin to increase the time you devote to activities, thereby increasing your concentration. For example, if you are an avid reader who can't seem to read for relaxation now, that's normal for people who experience grief and anxiety. You could dedicate yourself to reading for a set time and gradually increase it. You might also change the type of reading you do. For example, if you are an avid reader of mystery novels, I would suggest postponing that reading for now and instead delving into some feel-good stories. This approach would work well for other activities you have participated in or enjoyed in the past. If you used to exercise or walk a half hour a day, begin with ten minutes. Physical movement causes us to produce endorphins, the feel-good hormone. If you are less mobile, gentle stretching can help too. There are also how-to videos you can purchase or view on YouTube that show movement using a chair or other aid. One such public television show is *Sit and Be Fit with Mary Ann Wilson, RN*. These shows are for anyone who is less mobile and allow movement to be achieved using adjustments such as a chair.

Grieving can truly be exhausting. A grief journey can be lengthy, and it is normal for it to wax and wane. The pain may always be there, but it will soften, and you will adjust to the changes that the loss brought to you. This analogy shows how grief can wax and wane (Casabianca 2021): Visualize a bouncing ball inside of a closed box, and a push button inside the box. Your life is the closed box, and your grief is the bouncing ball. The push button inside the box generates the pain you feel from this loss. The bouncing ball in the box moves with every step you take. Sometimes, it hits the push button, which generates the pain you feel. Initially, the ball takes up most of the space in the box, so it will bounce into the button frequently.

When your loss first occurs, it may feel as if it encompasses every part of your being. Natural expressions of grief, crying or not crying, anger, sadness, and loneliness are frequent, and it feels like the pain of your grief will never end. You may feel like the huge ball leaves no room for anything else in your life, and it just plain hurts most of the time. Visualize that even though that ball is currently very large, it also has a tiny escape valve, and it will slowly lose air over time. As time passes, you may begin to experience grief as a smaller ball, which does not hit the push button for the pain as frequently. You may begin to engage in some of the things that you did before this difficult loss. As hard as this has been in your life, keep in mind that grief is still a bouncing ball. At times it may bounce off the walls in the box and hit the pain button again. This is how grief waxes and wanes. Grief has no timeline and can catch us by surprise. That is the nature of grief.

The grief ball does eventually become smaller. You will always miss your beloved pet who has died. As you adjust to life after the loss of your pet, it's important for you to have continued support from those who care about you. Continue to reach out and share the memories of your pet. Your beloved pet will always reside in a very special space in your heart filled with memories. Your grief impacts your life deeply and is ever-present. I hope this analogy gives you another way to understand grief. Grief never really goes away, and various triggers can bring it back to us in unexpected ways, at times when we least expect it. When that happens, it is important to be gentle with yourself. In any event, continue to give yourself time and a quiet space to reflect on your loss. Do not deny it. It is possible to feel peace after loss.

It is also important to understand that you need to reach out to a trained grief and loss counselor if the following are true:

- Your experiences frighten you.

- Your day-to-day life is adversely impacted in such a way that you are not able to get through the day and take care of yourself.

- You have these two concerns for more than a few days.

TAKE CARE OF YOURSELF FIRST

If you are also taking care of someone else, you need to take care of yourself first. You cannot help someone else if you are not in good enough shape to do it. If you take care of yourself first, you will be better able to take care of your other pets and people in your family.

If you have ever flown on an airplane, you have heard the oxygen mask presentation. The flight attendant says to put on your own mask first before helping someone else. You cannot help someone else with their mask if you pass out from insufficient oxygen.

EAT NUTRITIOUS FOOD AND KEEP HYDRATED

It is vital that you take care of yourself, so make sure you continue to meet your basic needs. It is very common to lose your appetite during grief. Your appetite may have left you, but the nutrition from healthy food is vital to your well-being. Smaller portions and more frequent eating of nutritious foods may work better for you. It may be helpful for you to purchase some protein drinks for limited-time use, but they are not really a long-term substitute for whole food. If someone asks if they can prepare something for you to eat, take them up on it. Be sure to continue eating and drinking adequate amounts of water.

Your journey through grief can be exhausting. It affects your mind, body, and spirit. It is always important to take care of yourself, but it is even more important during times of loss and grief. Eating too much, not enough, or unhealthy food might seem like a coping strategy, but, as you probably know, it will likely result in making you feel worse.

GET ADEQUATE SLEEP

You may have difficulty sleeping when you are grieving. However, you need to resist the urge to regularly nap during the day, so that you can have better sleep at night. Just as you prepare your body for sleep (putting on pajamas, brushing teeth, etc.), it is important to prepare your mind. Here are some tips that can help you do that:

- Maintain a regular sleep schedule.

- Avoid caffeine in the evening.

- Incorporate some relaxation techniques into your evening before bedtime.

- Turn down or turn off all electronic devices about an hour before you retire for the night.

- Do some gentle stretching.

- Connect with your spirituality by meditating or praying.

Be especially aware that the blue light from electronic devices interferes with your circadian (daily sleep/wake) rhythm, or sleep cycle. At night, it signals your brain to wake up when it should be winding down. In one study, as little as two hours of exposure to blue light at night slowed or stopped release of the sleep hormone, melatonin. Blue light emitted from your devices can keep you awake for *several hours* after you have stopped using them. To help prevent that, check your display settings on your mobile phone, tablet, or computer, and make sure the night light is turned on from sunset to sunrise. Using the night light will reduce the amount of blue in your display or screen and make it look like incandescent lighting ("warm white" or "soft white") instead of daylight.

CONNECT WITH NATURE AND NATURAL LIGHT

Connecting with nature can help you experience joy and allow for an immersion in the beauty of your surroundings. Experiences with nature can help stimulate your senses as you are exposed to a variety of soothing sights and sounds. If you live in an area where you experience the four seasons, you can soak up all the goodness of each season. You can appreciate each special feature, such as the warmth from the afternoon sun, the cool breezes, the crackle and colors of fallen leaves, and the softness of freshly fallen snow. You can learn from nature to be in the moment and appreciate the opportunity to relax and refocus. These promote stress-relieving feelings in our bodies.

Natural light helps our bodies produce vitamin D and ward off seasonal depression. It improves our circadian rhythm, which, in turn, helps us to regulate our sleep patterns.

TRY TO RELAX

After focusing on the basics—taking care of yourself first, eating nutritious food, and trying to get enough sleep—relaxing your body and mind can help ease your grief. Gradually incorporate some mind and body relaxation techniques into your daily routine. Here are some specific recommendations that have helped me and many of my clients practice self-care while grieving the loss of our pets.

Breathing Exercises

Breathing exercises can be extremely helpful for managing stress and anxiety. If you have a medical condition that affects your heart, lungs, or circulatory system, please check with your doctor first, to ask if breath work would be safe for you and whether you should make modifications. Here are a few breathing exercises to consider:

- When you start to feel the stress building, stop what you are doing, sit down if you can, take a deep breath in, and slowly release it. Close your eyes and focus on your breath and how your chest moves up and down. Then go back to what you were doing, and see if that was helpful. If so, remember to do it when the anxiety or inattention begins.

- Take a deep breath in through your nose, and then slowly release your breath through your pursed mouth, as if slowly blowing away bubbles. Then repeat as needed.

- Throughout the day, stop what you are doing and just sit quietly for one or two minutes. Now take in a deep breath and then slowly release it. Continue by taking in a full breath, and then exhale with an audible sigh (*aaahh*). Repeat, and with each exhalation let your shoulders drop and relax. Each time, inhale again and then release with the *aaahh* sound. Try it, and reap the benefits of relaxation.

Remember to be consistent in incorporating this breath work into your day. If you are interested in incorporating more breath work into your life, there are several books on this topic. One that I have used is *The Healing Power of the Breath* by Richard P. Brown, MD, and Patricia L. Gerbarg, MD (2012).

Good times to do breath work are first thing in the morning and just before bed. In the morning, it will refresh you and bring you some calmness as you start your day. In the evening, it can help relax you for sleep.

Visual Imagery

When using visual imagery to calm yourself, quiet music and a peaceful setting will enhance your experience. It also helps to dim the lighting or even use candles. Eliminate distractions and wrap yourself in a blanket for warmth and a feeling of safety. You can focus on a peaceful scene you have in your mind's eye or physically place a picture of one in front of you. As you begin, take some calming breaths or engage in the sample breathing exercises above. Look at the picture and focus on the happy memories and moments you experienced in the location of that picture.

I have a memory I always can pull up in my mind of a peaceful bubbling brook in Vermont. I can close my eyes, see the brook, and hear the water in my mind. I can stay in that space for a while, then open my eyes and feel content and calm. There are also apps for your phone that can walk you through a visual imaginary experience, as well as YouTube videos. There are also books that have visual scripts that you can read or have someone else read and record for your use.

Mindfulness

Mindfulness is all about staying in the present moment. You can practice mindfulness as you go about your daily life. It can slow you down and make you appreciate and be more aware of life. For example, try mindful walking. Make an effort to enjoy what you see, smell, and feel. Feel the differences in the surfaces you are walking on, such as grass or concrete. Notice the trees, flowers, and other objects you encounter. Get up close to a flower, really look at it, and marvel at its beauty. There is so much to take in, and each walk along the same path will be different. Avoid distractions like your cell phone. Keep it in your pocket for safety.

When you are outside in a quiet space, notice the warmth of the sun on your face, feel the wind blow through, and just be with yourself quietly. I remember the wind being an inspiration for me in creating a name for a gazebo in my mom's memory. Being in the present can slow you down, bring calmness to your life, and even help the creative juices to flow.

Another example is mindful eating. Take a bite of food, and notice things you had not noticed before—is it salty, sweet, or crunchy?

Positive Affirmations

Positive affirmations are phrases or thoughts that you can write down on paper and later read and reflect upon. They can help you focus on a positive feeling if you read them out loud and repeat them often. An example is: "I have been through a devastating loss in my life, but I am grateful for my support system."

You can create your own messages or find them in books or on websites that feature positive affirmations. You can also use quotes or phrases that have meaning for you and inspire you to feel more positive. There are many quotes throughout this book. If one or more of them really resonates with you, copy it down on attractive paper or a colorful index card, and read it daily.

Musical Relaxation

Record or purchase some music that makes you feel calm when you hear it. It is important to not use music that you normally hear at work or listen to on a regular basis. That can trigger thoughts of past events that may have been stressful. Get into a relaxing, comfortable chair or space and close your eyes. Put a warm, moist facecloth on your eyes or forehead, and just focus on your breath and the music in your ears.

Coloring Experience

Many adult coloring books are available in stores and online. They come in many topics. You can find them with flower themes, design themes, bird themes, mandalas, and so much more. Coloring can calm the fear center in your brain. It can help reduce the intrusive thoughts in your mind and switch off other unwanted thoughts so that you can focus on the moment. Coloring can give you the same calming effect you receive while meditating. Invest in a good-quality set of colored pencils, markers, or crayons, and enjoy the moments.

EMBRACE SOCIAL OPPORTUNITIES

Many of my clients have found it helpful to formally set aside time to grieve in their own way and release some of their emotions surrounding this loss. If we don't find ways to release these intense emotions, they can have a very unsettling way of building up inside of us. The buildup may cause us to lash out at others, even if we don't normally do this. Sometimes it's like a slow release through a valve with our emotions; gently let them out when you feel safe, supported, and in friendly surroundings. Sharing your feelings with caring and understanding people in your life can help you create the space for formal grieving, as well as being extremely beneficial to you as you grieve. Ask family, friends, neighbors, and members of your faith community, if you have one, whether they would be willing to lend a supportive ear. If you belong to a faith community, they may have prayer groups or prayer circles.

If you are invited out for dinner or coffee, be open to the opportunity, focus on the person you are with, and enjoy their company. Realizing it can be difficult at times to push through the day, it is important that you continue to try. Connecting with others who have common interests with you can go a long way in helping you through your grief and keeping you engaged in life.

EXERCISE

Movement, stretching, or light exercise routines in which you normally engage are helpful. They can also help you get more restful sleep. However, please avoid strenuous exercise before bed, as that can keep you awake longer.

TALK OR WRITE ABOUT YOUR LOSS

While physically talking to others is one way of expressing your feelings, it is not always possible to have someone nearby who is available to share your feelings. Another way to help uncover your thoughts is through journaling; it can be a very effective tool when you need to vent and sort through your emotions. When you want to engage in journaling, first find a comfortable quiet space. You may want to add some quiet music. When writing in a journal, there is no need for proper spelling or grammar. This is a place for your unfiltered thoughts. One of the goals is to let the feelings come out in words. Let the words flow from your heart to the pen and onto the paper. If you feel overwhelmed by them, reach out to a trusted person for their support. Sometimes, stopping for a few minutes and taking some deep breaths can ease your anxious thoughts. So can stretching, thinking of a happy memory, or holding a special memento in your hand. You may also wish to do some journaling using art materials.

Reading through your journal at a later time and reflecting

can shed light on what you have been through and how you got to this point. You always have the choice to keep this journal private or share parts of it with trusted others.

You are introduced to writing experiences at the end of each chapter. As with the other suggestions in this chapter, there may be some that speak to you and you want to try right away, and you may wish to try others at another time. You can choose to engage with them now or later when you feel they may be more helpful to you.

Consider a Support Group

A support group can provide you with a listening and welcoming venue to share your grief with others who are experiencing the loss of a pet. Sharing your experience of loss can be helpful to you, and also to the people hearing your story. Sharing feelings can help you know that people understand and care and that you are not alone. Grief support groups provide beneficial support to each person in the group and can offer new coping skills to assist in your grief journey. Group sharing can also help you see how others have walked their own path of grief.

If you join a support group, you may not feel like sharing right away, and that is okay. Maybe in time you will feel comfortable enough to do so. If you feel it will be helpful, it can be very worthwhile to try.

Support groups can be open or closed. An open group allows interested people to drop in on the meetings at any time, and they are ongoing. A closed group is only available to people who sign up in advance, and are held for a predetermined length of time. Some have a fixed agenda, while others are for ad hoc sharing; some may be a combination of the two. Groups can be facilitated by volunteers, peers, or a professional grief and loss counselor.

Each group is different, and if you don't feel comfortable in one group, you may find another one that is more helpful to you. You can check with your vet, your local humane society, a local pet cemetery, or friends and family to see if any are available in your area.

Find a Grief Counselor

At some point throughout your journey of grief, you may begin to feel stuck. You may feel your grief has become more complicated and you don't feel that you can adequately work through your emotions without professional assistance. It's okay to reach out for help. There is no shame or stigma in doing so.

A counselor or therapist can support you through many concerns, including grief and loss, life stressors, transitions, and anxiety. Some issues may have surfaced for you since the loss of your pet and need to be addressed. It is a big step if you are seeking the assistance of a grief counselor; congratulate yourself and continue to move forward.

Here are suggestions for how to begin the process of finding a therapist. I recommend having a notebook to gather information throughout the process. Using a notebook will also allow you to bring it with you to your actual session(s) with any questions or concerns you want to discuss. For each potential counselor, start by jotting down the name, location, phone number or email address, and any other information that is helpful to you in deciding whether this counselor is someone you may be interested in contacting to set up an initial phone consultation. Many counselors offer a free brief phone call so that both of you can ask questions to see if this professional relationship would be a good fit for you. A "good fit" should include affirmative answers to the following questions: "Do I feel comfortable talking with this person?" and

"If I continue to work with this person, do I feel they can help me sort through my concerns?"

If you are employed, check with your human resources department to find out if you have access to a benefit called an employee assistance program, or EAP. They would have a listing of counselors in the area that are available to you. You could be referred to one or more of them for a fixed number of visits, free of charge, as one of your employee benefits. When you reach the limit, you can choose to continue with this therapist or go to a different one. Then you would use your insurance coverage, if the therapist accepts this insurance, or pay out-of-pocket for continued services.

If you do not have an employee assistance program, there are many other ways that you can find a counselor:

- The website of your health insurance carrier may have a listing of counselors who are "in network."

- Depending on your comfort level for sharing with family or friends, you may want to share with them that you are considering seeking out grief counseling. You can ask them if they know of a counselor in your area.

- You can ask your medical professionals to recommend a grief counselor.

- *Psychology Today* provides a directory of counselors and also allows users to select and sort them by insurance, types of therapy utilized, location, and price (https://www.psychologytoday.com/us/therapists).

- You can search online for therapists in your area as well, and then follow up by checking their website or other listings.

- If you decide to seek out a counselor who has experience specifically with pet grief and loss, you can ask your veterinarian or an emergency veterinary service.

Factors in selecting a suitable counselor include:

❖ How can I pay for this service?

❖ Do I have a preference for a gender-specific counselor?

❖ Do I want a counselor who offers secure online counseling, or do I prefer in-person office visits?

Once you have some names, you can then research them online to see if they have a website. Therapists with websites will generally have information that can help you become familiar with their practice, such as their location, types of conditions they counsel people for, particular training they have, specialties they treat, insurance plans they accept, and types of therapies they use (such as cognitive behavioral therapy, or CBT).

You will find several different types of professionals who counsel, including mental health counselors, social workers, marriage and family therapists, psychologists, psychiatrists, and psychiatric nurse practitioners. It is very important to find an individual who is licensed; in some states, not all professionals are licensed. There are also faith-based or spiritual-based counselors. For grief and loss counseling, most individuals will not need the services of a psychiatrist or psychiatric nurse practitioner.

Licensed mental health counselors (LMHC) have gone through advanced training in mental health counseling and have passed a licensing exam in their state that allows them to practice mental health counseling. Other states use similar names, such as licensed clinical counselor (LCC) or licensed professional counselor (LPC). Social workers have similar initials after their names, such as LMSW or LCSW. Both mental health counselors and social workers have a master's degree and continue their education beyond that with additional training and classes. They also have formal supervised internships before they can work independently in their own practices. Additional initials after names can refer to any specific training or expertise they may have. Titles may differ outside the United States.

At Your First Appointment

Now that you have made that very important call and followed through with making an appointment, congratulations! If this is the first time you have met with a counselor, you may feel a little apprehensive. Yes, it can be scary and a little anxiety provoking, so here are a few tips as you prepare for this important meeting.

- Arrive a few minutes before your scheduled time.

- Do some basic breathing exercises.

- Have your small notebook of questions and concerns with you.

- Give yourself some downtime in your schedule after the session so you can absorb the information and be alone with your thoughts.

Choosing a professional counselor who has the appropriate education and training is very important, but equally important is feeling that this person actively listens to you and your concerns and that you feel comfortable and validated. Respect your gut feeling and ask questions like "Is it a good fit for me to work with this person?" and "Do I feel they can be helpful to me in my situation?" The most important part of therapy is the therapeutic alliance between you and your counselor. Entering into therapy is a cooperative venture. You will have to work together to help you through your concerns. Taking the time to consider the information that is provided will help to make your experience a rewarding one.

ESTABLISH A NEW ROUTINE AND SET GOALS

After the death or loss of your pet, you will find that your routine is upside down. You and your pet grew around a routine from waking up in the morning to retiring at night. A good balance between following a daily or weekly routine and achieving goals can be very helpful to keep you moving along with more purpose. If you stopped following your routine after the death of your pet, establish a new one. When you are in the grips of grief, having both a routine and daily goals can help you get some structure and control over your day, but don't overdo it. Processing grief can be draining. Allow for some time to rest and regroup. Decide if a new routine might be something that can help now or in the future.

Every morning, as part of your routine, set a goal for the day. After a week or two, if you are feeling up to it, increase it to two goals, and later increase to three. In the beginning stages of your grief, you may need something as simple as "I will get out of bed, shower, and get dressed. I will nourish my body with healthy food, and I will venture outside for natural light." In the evening, take a few minutes to reflect on what you have accomplished. Give yourself a pat on the back for what you have done, in light of what you are experiencing with your grief. Recognize that nobody completes every goal every day; tomorrow is another opportunity. Some days will be a little easier for you, and others will feel like you are moving through quicksand. Keep in mind that the most important thing is to keep moving, as each passing day will bring more relief from your anguish. Don't forget to include activities you enjoy, such as hobbies, gardening, and whatever else brings some joy into your life.

One way to find a balance in your life while grieving is to alternately choose times of solitude for yourself and times when you are in the company of others who can validate your loss. Solitude includes time alone to rest your body and mind.

Attend to your body by moving and stretching. If you have been regularly taking part in physical activity, refer back to the list earlier in this chapter. You may want to consider temporarily replacing your current workout methodology with something different. When you are grieving, it can be beneficial to disengage from activities that remind you of your loss and choose others instead. For example, perhaps you followed your workout by cuddling and playing with your pet. Even a relatively minor change to your routine may lessen your acute sense of loss and help provide a respite from your grief. A new activity may also give you a little gentle nudge to engage in it and begin to enjoy it.

Since grief can present itself physically, it can be very helpful to participate in some type of physical movement activity, like yoga. Yoga is a total mind-body workout that includes deep breathing, meditation, and relaxation exercises. Many benefits can be obtained from practicing yoga, including releasing physical and emotional tension in our bodies. This is helpful when working through grief.

There are many types of yoga, such as power yoga, restorative yoga, kundalini yoga, and grief yoga. You can practice some types with the aid of a chair, as I found out after taking a class in restorative yoga. Grief yoga is also offered in my local area, and it may be offered in yours too. Additionally, there are several books on grief yoga available. It is not necessary to attend a group yoga session, as yoga can be practiced by yourself at home by using instructional videos.

When you are in the company of others, reach out to trusted listeners who can validate your feelings, and keep your distance from others who do not understand. If you are employed, you might have vacation or personal time off to allow you to focus on decompressing from this loss.

EXPRESS GRATITUDE

Throughout your day, try to focus on the positive things that are happening, as this will allow your body to experience a different emotion. This, in turn, can bring you out from under the pain you are experiencing into a state of gratitude for all the wonderful times you spent with your cherished pet. It may be difficult to embrace gratitude in the face of your grief, but gratitude can really coexist with grief. As you peel through the layers of your grief, gradually embracing and expressing gratitude can aid in your healing. For example, you can reflect on the memories you made with your pet by writing about them and expressing your gratitude for them. As a pet guardian, you already know how much your pet brought to your life. My dog Jazzy has taught me many things, including the very important need to stretch (especially as I work on this book!). Watching her stretch encourages me to stretch too.

Writing can help you reminisce and express unfiltered thoughts and feelings. It can also serve as a means of release and a way to honor the life of your beloved pet. Expressing gratitude can be a powerful means of helping you through your grief and allowing you to embrace hope for the days ahead.

REFLECTIVE WRITING EXPERIENCES

CHAPTER 9:

Taking Care of You

*"There are three needs of the griever:
To find the words for the loss, to say the words aloud
and to know that the words have been heard."*

—VICTORIA ALEXANDER

Refer back to the introduction for the specifics on completing the writing experiences in this book. I recommend the use of a notebook reserved for this purpose so that you can review and reflect on your thoughts later.

Writing Experience—Taking Care of You

Looking back at the ideas in this chapter, can you choose one thing that you can focus on to take care of you? Take out your notebook and write it in bold lettering. Every day from now on, write about how it felt to do this and if you felt it was helpful. Also write down any changes or adaptations you make specifically for yourself. Commit to at least one thing you will incorporate into your life going forward. Remember, changes take time.

Next week, try adding one or two additional activities. Commit to doing them on a consistent basis. Later on, keep trying to add different ones to your daily life or change some of the others.

I hope you will gain some relaxation and peace.

"*Birds will always sing a song for those that they love.*"

—ANTHONY T. HINCKS

Chapter 10

Helping Others Who Are Grieving with You

veryone who knew, loved, and engaged with your pet is grieving from this loss. The information in this chapter can help you to help others who are grieving along with you. It can also be used by someone who is supporting a person who is grieving, such as a friend who is not a member of the family.

If you feel at this time that you cannot be emotionally available to others experiencing this loss, it is okay if you need to skip this chapter for now in order to focus on yourself. If another person in your family is struggling, it would be helpful to seek out another family member or trusted friend to work with them on their grief. For example, if it is a child, someone can read an age-appropriate story to them on pet loss and use the story to relate to their loss.

The age, relationship with the pet, and current life situation of those grieving along with you affects their grief. Accordingly, each person's grief needs to be addressed separately. For a child, this may be the first time they are experiencing grief, or maybe one of your children is away from home and had a deep relationship with the family pet.

Acknowledging Their Loss

It is never easy to know what to say to someone who is grieving. The way to do it is to acknowledge their loss, and let them know that if they'd like to talk about it, you are there to listen. Words like "I know that this is a difficult time for you, losing [pet's name]" are a good place to start. Asking them to tell you about the pet who passed, so that they know you are a willing listener, can also be a good way to start the conversation. Be sure to refer to the pet by name so that your inquiry is personalized and acknowledges the importance of the loss.

Asking the person who is grieving to share some experiences with the pet who is gone can be very helpful to them. I lost my dog Wishbone over ten years ago, and to this day, when I share something about him, it always lights up my face with a smile. I experience a rush of feelings of joy and thankfulness that he was in our lives for sixteen years. I will always remember his silly antics, the laughter he brought to my life, and his own unique way of comforting me through difficult times. I miss him. My cherished memories of him will always live in my heart.

You can ask, "Tell me one of the really silly things [pet's name] did," "What are some of your favorite memories of [pet's name]?" and "I know [pet's name] was very precious to you." Again, always use the pet's name when remembering and talking about them.

There are also some things that are better not said when people are grieving, such as "We can always get another pet" and "You should be over this by now."

LISTENING

"The most basic and powerful way to connect to another person is to listen. Just listen."

—RACHEL NAOMI REMEN

Sometimes just listening can be immensely helpful. You can ask them to tell you about the pet who has died. Here are some questions to start the conversation:

- Can you share with me some of the funniest times you remember about [pet's name]?
- What made [pet's name] so special to you?

Focusing on the positive aspects of their relationship can be very therapeutic, but listening is the key.

Unfortunately, we cannot take away their pain, but listening unconditionally and being present can help with their healing. If they are able to get out and about, you might want to suggest they attend a support group on pet grief and loss. There may be other grief support resources in your area that you can find out about and share with them as well. You can check with a local veterinary office for possible resources, or do some research on your own.

SENDING EXPRESSIONS OF CONCERN

A card or a special note can be very meaningful to someone who no longer resides in your household but is experiencing the loss of the family pet. Maybe a family member is away at college or living independently. Email and text messages can be helpful too, but sometimes a card that you can hold and display, or put in a memory book or box, can have a more profound effect on someone who is grieving. Many cards are specific to the loss of a pet, both at stores and online. Additionally, expressing your own sentiments in a handwritten note card can be very healing. You may also wish to try your hand at creating one yourself. There are many possible sentiments that you can add, or just express that you know this has been a difficult time, add their pet's name, and include a happy memory of them.

When you sense that the person who is grieving is ready, you might bring up the topic of how to memorialize the pet, and share with them some of the ideas in this book. That material can go a long way in helping them along their grief journey. Checking on them once in a while would be a wonderful gesture on your part.

HELPING CHILDREN

Children understand and experience death differently at different developmental stages. Please seek additional information from your child's teacher or pediatrician to further help them at a specific age range, developmental stage, or circumstance. This will improve your support for that particular child.

When children lose a cherished pet, it may be their first experience with loss. Please don't say the family pet was "put to sleep." It is very important to be honest about death and reassure your child. Be there for your child during this time of grief. It is important to touch base with them often and ask how they feel. You may wish to check out books for children on grief and loss, listed in Appendix A. A book can help open the door to understanding that all living beings die.

My first experience with death as a child was when a family

pet named Skippy vanished from my life. I was a very young child, maybe four or five years old. I remember Skippy very well; he was a beautiful brown-and-black beagle mix who lived with my aunt and uncle. I looked forward to visiting my aunt and uncle so I could see and interact with Skippy. I was a little tyke, but oh, how I remember him! One time, my family and I visited my aunt and uncle and, unfortunately, Skippy was not there. I don't remember any conversation about him, only that he was gone, and I missed the love he showered on me. I never was able to find out what happened to Skippy, who provided me with my first experience of love and loss for a pet. I do know that he left good memories in my heart, and I love a picture I have of him. As an adult, I often wonder what happened to Skippy. I feel sad to this day because I never found out. So please, always be straightforward with your child about your pet's passing, with honesty and age-appropriate information. Reassure your child that you are there for them.

Inform Teachers or Other Caregivers

It is equally important to let teachers or other caregivers know that your family pet, or a pet your child was close to, has died. They are in a position to notice and understand any changes in your child's behavior or mood. These may need to be addressed, as your child will need understanding and continued support during their grief journey and the subsequent changes in their life. A teacher or caregiver may schedule time for reading about pet loss or talking about the topic, especially if they have been informed that a child in the class has lost a pet.

Helpful Age-Appropriate Books

In my first career as an educator of children, I was frequently informed of the loss of a family pet and some of the effects it was having on the child. I had one or two favorite books in my collection that I would read to the class on this topic. Sometimes we would follow up with a lesson on pets in our lives and a subsequent art activity. It provided an opportunity for the children to ask questions and express their feelings for past and present losses. There are many wonderful books available to help explain the death of a pet to children and to deal with loss. Some of them are listed in Appendix A at the end of this book. You can also ask a librarian or a teacher for age-appropriate books on pet grief and loss.

Other Support for Children

This can be a very scary time for children, and they can experience many different emotions, including anger, guilt, and sadness.

Other supportive people in your children's lives may be helpful at this time, as you may also be feeling overwhelmed by this loss. As mentioned previously, it can be very helpful to reach out to your children's current teachers, or previous teachers that they connected with, and let them know of the loss of your pet. They can notice any changes during the course of the school day, speak privately with your child(ren), and alert you to anything they notice.

It can be helpful to your own healing and that of your child(ren) to share a story of pets you lost when you were growing up, how you felt, and what you did to help you with your sadness. You might ask them if they would like a picture of the pet in their room, with a small battery-operated candle near it. It's important to not feel that you have to hide your emotions while you are grieving. Perhaps there is a particularly close family member— such as a grandparent, aunt, uncle, or cousin—who lost a cherished pet when they were young; they can speak about this loss and how they experienced and coped with it. If there are other family members or friends who do not fully understand the impact your pet had on your life, it may also be helpful for you to speak with them and explain to them that this is a very difficult and sad time for you and your children, and ask for their understanding.

With your support, and the support of everyone who loves them, children can get through to the other side of their loss. In time, they can find some comfort knowing that their cherished pet lives on in their hearts. In other words, they will come to have some acceptance of this death in their lives. It is helpful and healing for them to be included in any type of goodbye ceremony or memorial to honor this cherished pet. Chapter 11 contains some activities that can be done with children.

HELPING ADOLESCENTS

Peer support is very important to adolescents, but they are still looking for support from their parents and other trusted adults in their lives. Adolescents are still trying to find their way and understand their many emotions. It may be very difficult for them to express their true feelings. One day they react like a young child and need a lot of reassurance, and the next day it can be "What's the big deal?" They can become hyperemotional or show a total lack of concern. What's important is to let them know that, if they want to talk about their pet's death, you are there for them and you will listen.

". . . Perhaps the most important thing we ever give each other is our attention. . . . A loving silence often has far more power to heal and to connect than the most well-intentioned words."

—RACHEL NAOMI REMEN

HELPING YOUNG ADULTS

Perhaps they have gone off to college or moved away from the family home. They may have had a very close relationship with the deceased pet and feel guilty about abandoning the pet that has been in their life since they were very young. Let them know that you, as their parent or family member, are there for them, to really listen and share in their tears. Don't be afraid to share with them that this is a harsh reality of life when we lose a precious family pet. Discuss some things you can do together to celebrate all the good memories. Since they are away from home, the gesture of sending them a note in the mail, a text message, or even a small care package can help them to feel loved and cared for.

HELPING OTHER FAMILY PETS THAT ARE ALSO GRIEVING

Did you know that animals also grieve the loss of another animal? Barbara King, a professor of anthropology and the author of *How Animals Grieve*, sheds light on this very interesting topic. She states, "They're bonded like us." She further asserts in a special *Time* issue: "We are all socially attuned, and in many ways our brains are even wired similarly. Why wouldn't animals mourn?" (King 2014).

Many clients have recounted stories to me of their surviving pets' behaviors after losing a fellow pet buddy. This chapter includes some of the important things you can do for your surviving pets, as well as some of the behaviors they may display. Animals truly do miss and grieve other animals that were in their lives. They even have mourning rituals. For example, cats repeatedly visit a home where a now-deceased companion cat used to live.

We know that dogs exhibit social behavior, and when there is a loss of a group member, the surviving dogs may have a hard time coping with and adjusting to the loss. The pet that died might have provided important knowledge and guidance to the group, and the surviving pets may be confused until one of them takes over that role. Be patient while the surviving pets in your home work this out. Like humans, individual dogs and cats react differently to family loss. Look for signs of grief in your family pets, such as acting withdrawn, whining or howling in dogs, and crying in cats. Other pets may pace around or search the house for the deceased pet. There may be a change in their bathroom or grooming habits, particularly in cats. They may also have less of an appetite and not get enough hydration. Check on these things for the sake of their health.

If your pet begins to exhibit some unwelcome signs of hurting, such as howling or other unwanted behaviors, it may be best to ignore them for a while and wait until they have settled down a bit. We don't want to reward bad behavior, but on the other hand, we want to comfort them. Once they have settled down a bit, we can offer our reassurance and plenty of attention. If they have a favorite activity, like playing ball with you, now would be a good time to engage in it. The loss of a pet is a major transition for the whole family, so remember to provide comfort to any surviving pets in the household. It is important to consult with your veterinarian if you have any other concerns, and especially if you see your pet exhibiting continued physical or emotional signs of distress.

Make a commitment to yourself to spend extra quality time with your other pets. Maybe you could take a longer walk with them, and engage in activities with them that they previously enjoyed. Maybe you could do some extra special grooming that they enjoy. They can always benefit from more playtime and cuddling. Taking your pet to a special place they enjoy or to visit another pet whose company they enjoy can be helpful to them during their grief.

Remember that working through grief can be exhausting. As a result of this loss, there will be changes in everyone's life.

CHAPTER 10:

Helping Others Who Are Grieving with You
Writing Experience—Commit to Helping Someone Else in Their Grief

Did something you read in this chapter speak to you about how you can help someone else? Is there someone in your family who is also dealing with grief from this loss whom you might be able to help? There are so many ways we can reach out and help others.

Write down something you feel you can do to help someone else in your family circle who is also grieving, and list some ways you can put this help into motion. Whatever you choose to do, remember that hugs can go a long way toward easing the grief you are all experiencing. If you feel that at this time you cannot immediately help someone else, be kind to yourself and know that in time you may be able to extend yourself in that direction. Be gentle and kind to yourself, and ask someone else to check on that person and engage with them in their grief.

Your gift of time and attention to someone else in need can have a very positive impact on their life.

"A pet is never truly forgotten until
it is no longer remembered."

—LACIE PETITTO

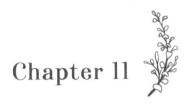

Chapter 11

Remembering and Honoring Your Pet

ourning a pet will take time. Honoring them with gratitude for the wonderful memories you shared together can help you heal from grief. Memories keep the past alive, and they link the past to the present. You can no longer see, hear, or touch your pet, but they will always be in your heart and memories.

There are many therapeutic ways to honor and memorialize a beloved pet. This chapter has many activities that can be done individually or as a group. They have helped many people in my professional practice, including children, older adults, and families. Choose what you would like to do now, and then come back to engage in something else later. You could do something on the anniversary of the day they came into your life. You can also do something on the anniversary of their death, their birthday, or on no particular day. Fill the day with gratitude for their having been in your life. Choose something that will have special meaning for you and bring you peace and comfort. None of the activities on these pages require any special talent, so please try one, as they can be very healing. Full details are given for the following:

- 🐾 Preparing and circulating an obituary

- 🐾 Setting aside a special location for the pet's remains

- Conducting a memorial service

- Writing a variety of documents

- Placing a memorial stone, plant, or tree in a special place

- Making a memorial donation

- Volunteering

- Making a variety of things with one's own hands

- Producing a memorial website or PowerPoint presentation

- Producing a memorial video

We can celebrate the lives and memories that were made and know that our pet will always have a special place reserved in our hearts. Let us honor them with gratitude for the many wonderful ways that they enhanced our lives, the fun and silly times, the loyalty, the unconditional love, and the companionship. Take some time to reflect on the life that was shared by you and your beloved pet. Memories keep the past alive by linking it to the present.

Discuss as a family other ways to honor your beloved pet's memory at special events or holidays. For example, if you celebrate Christmas, you might want to create or purchase a special ornament with your pet's name on it and place it on the tree every year. Another idea for a Christmas item is, if you always hung a stocking for your pet, you can still do that, but fill it with items that can be donated to an animal-related cause.

As mentioned in the previous chapter, it is very important to include children in the process of grieving. Here are some suggestions that you might want to do individually, with children, or with your entire family.

Obituary

You may want to write an obituary for your pet. In the past, many have submitted obituaries for circulation in their local newspaper, but there are not very many local newspapers left. However, there are other printed publications that may be appropriate. Many breed and rescue newsletters accept memorial or obituary articles for little or no cost. For example, *True Grit*, the magazine of the Jack Russell Terrier Club of America, accepts them from members on a space-available basis. Alternatively, you may write one and post it on your Facebook page or other social media site. It can also be written just for you, or for others, and placed in a small frame or memory book.

Locations for Your Pet's Remains

If your pet was cremated, and you have their remains in an urn, you can set aside a special place in your home for them. Some suggestions are a bookcase shelf, a mantel, or burial in a special place. If you place the urn in your home, a framed picture of your pet beside the urn can make for a meaningful remembrance. When my Wishbone passed, I hung his collar with his name tag over his picture frame.

If your pet's remains are to be scattered, a meaningful place where your pet liked to walk or play may be a good choice. However, be sure to check if there are any restrictions in your area about scattering remains.

If your pet was buried, a memory stone can be placed at the area where they are buried or in some other special place. Many regions have pet cemeteries. Ask for suggestions from family members so they all feel a part of this and know that their thoughts and feelings are important.

Memorial Service

You can hold a memorial service for your pet. Each person in attendance might light a candle in your pet's memory. Consider inviting others who have been a part of your pet's life to share in this service. Each person can be invited to celebrate your pet's life by sharing a special memory that can be written down and spoken aloud. The written memories can be stored in a special box or placed in a scrapbook and then reread at another time.

WRITING ACTIVITIES

Writing can be very helpful in clearing our minds and helping us to express our feelings. Writing a story, making a journal entry, or writing a creative poem can facilitate healing and bring some peace. Check back on the writing experiences at the end of each chapter; if you have not yet engaged with them, now might be a good time.

Create a Book

Individually or as a family, put together a simple book about your life with your pet. You can start out with a picture of your pet, and include pages with some of these topics:

- How and why was your pet's name chosen?
- How did you feel the first time you saw this pet and why?
- What were their physical characteristics (color, breed, markings, size)?
- What was your daily or weekly routine like with this pet?
- What special activities did you enjoy together?

🐾 Was there a special place your pet liked to hang out?

🐾 Did they have interesting and funny antics?

What was your pet's favorite treat or human food? My dogs always loved raw carrots. I used to call Wishbone "Veggie Dog" because he loved carrots, cooked broccoli, green beans, and sweet potatoes. When I think of that, it brings a smile to my face, and a few chuckles.

If you create a book, you can also create a cover for your book. You can purchase a special scrapbook from a craft store or use a binder. This book can be enjoyed for many years to come, and serve as a reminder of all of the special times with your cherished pet. Take it out on a special day, or any day that you are particularly remembering your beloved pet. It can help to remind you to focus on your special pet with gratitude for all of the memories you shared together. Remember, our memories cannot be taken away from us, and yours will always connect you to your cherished pet and the life you shared. Your pet lives on in your heart with your shared experiences, and you can celebrate a life well lived.

Write a Poem

How about writing a simple poem about your pet? A particular type of poem that you might want to try is haiku. This is a Japanese verse form that consists of three unrhymed lines of five, seven, and five syllables. Haiku often features an image, or a pair of images, meant to depict the essence of a specific moment in time. You can brainstorm some words about your pet or your feelings, either by yourself or with your family, and then write a haiku to share.

Here is a sample haiku for my dog Wishbone written by my son, Steven. He is memorializing several things about him:

- 🐾 "Treetop" is the name of the kennel he is from.
- 🐾 "Sump Pump" refers to his obsession with barking and growling at the sump pump whenever it ran.
- 🐾 "Mister MacPooch" is a nickname for him that originated in an episode of the 1990s PBS show *Wishbone*, which was about a Jack Russell terrier.
- 🐾 "Go To Ground" is an event at a Jack Russell terrier trial, at which Wishbone did quite well—as well as an allegory for death itself.

Treetop Wishbone Dog
Sump Pump Mister MacPooch Dog
Go To Ground, Good Boy

OUTDOOR ACTIVITIES

If you have a home with space for a new tree or a special flowering bush, you can plant one in your pet's memory. You can always add a special plant to your existing garden. Every time you see the blooms on the tree or bush, you can think of new life emerging in memory of your beloved pet.

Placing a memorial stone with your pet's name on it is a nice addition to your remembrance of your pet. It can be placed in a garden or by the new tree or flowering bush. When Wishbone passed, I purchased a large stone with his name on it and placed it under the tree that he always ran around chasing squirrels. I also found a small ceramic figure of his breed and placed it near the memorial stone.

If you don't have a yard, you can always purchase a special indoor plant in your pet's memory, locate it in a special place in your home, and add a picture.

Monetary Donations

If your finances allow you to make a donation in your pet's name to a particular pet shelter or animal cause, that can be a great way to honor your pet's memory. If your pet died from a specific disease, and there is an organization that is researching a cure, you might like to donate to that research. Several animal research organizations maintain a database of animals affected by certain diseases, both inherited and otherwise, in the well-founded hope that it will help them to find a cure, a better treatment for the disease, or the knowledge required to breed it out of the animals' bloodlines. The elimination of a certain type of hereditary deafness in Jack Russell terriers is one such success story. If that situation is applicable to your pet (your vet or national breed organization would know), submitting his or her information to one of these databases will be quite valuable. The knowledge that you are helping to eliminate one or more of these horrible diseases would be a most fitting tribute to your pet.

Something to consider when making a donation to a US organization is to verify the organization's 501©(3) status, to ensure that your donations can be itemized as a charitable donation on your tax return. This can be done via a search of the IRS website at https://www.irs.gov/charities-non-profits/tax-exempt-organization-search. Also, many state attorneys general compile information regarding the percentage of donations to a particular charity that actually goes toward the cause championed by the charity. Give strong preference to an organization that uses less than 10 to 20 percent of its money for fundraising.

MEMORIAL BENCHES AND OTHER ITEMS

Many humane societies and other animal care and advocacy organizations accept donations for memorial benches, bricks on maintained trails, and other suitable items for use by visitors to their facilities and the animals being housed. Many of these can include a memorial plaque with your pet's and your family's name if you wish.

VOLUNTEER OPPORTUNITIES

We each have different talents and interests, and we all have the power to make a difference in others' lives. Giving back is a wonderfully rewarding way to honor the memory of your pet. Perhaps a volunteer experience is something that would interest you.

You may donate some of your time to volunteer in a local animal shelter or work on fundraising for the organization. Many breeds, species (not just dogs and cats), and geographical areas have rescue organizations. If your pet came from a rescue organization, you could volunteer to help out by fostering an animal in transition or providing other assistance in kind. You could spend some time with animals in shelters by taking them on walks, playing with them, and showing them your love by petting or grooming them. Your time is worth a lot, and the care you give to other animals can be a wonderful gift to them.

I will always treasure the heartfelt message I received from a past client, who had initially come to me with the devastating news that her beloved dog had just died. Years later, she reconnected with me. It was wonderful to read her message of thanks for my help through this loss, but it warmed me even more to learn of her volunteer experience, as we had discussed that as a possibility. She felt it had helped to reach out to other pets in need. She knew she made a difference in their lives, even if it was for only a few hours a week. She volunteered at a pet rescue organization, where she walked and played with dogs awaiting adoption. She told me about how much this experience has helped her to realize how important it is to give back. She could see the difference in the dogs she interacted with after their walks and playtimes. She felt that she was the lucky one, to be able to make this difference in their lives and honor her dog's memory. In her heart, she knew her dog would tell her, "Great job and thanks for helping to get them out in the fresh air."

Like my past client, you may still want to have a pet in your life that you can interact with on your own schedule, whether daily or weekly. Volunteering at a shelter or other facility will allow you to be with animals without bringing them into your home to live. Walking dogs for animal shelters can be most rewarding. Not only are you providing exercise for the animal, but you are getting exercise for yourself and helping them with their socialization skills. That can allow them to go up for adoption sooner. You can also volunteer indirectly, working on behalf of animal causes through advocacy, fundraising, and adoption from animal shelters. The correct decision is the one that works for your current situation.

A closer-to-home choice might be to walk your neighbor's dog or look after their family pet when they travel.

Another option is animal-assisted activities (AAA), which involve planned casual meetings with people in need. They bring comfort and recreation to those in long-term facilities, patients receiving cancer or other medical treatment, and people dealing with anxiety. Various organizations offer training for volunteers to go out with trained therapy dogs, cats, and other domestic animals, to visit a variety of institutions, assisted living facilities, children's hospitals, nursing homes, and schools. You can help with a pet-assisted visit through a local organization that supervises and facilitates bringing pets to people who need a visit from a furry or feathery friend. This is something I found very helpful and rewarding after my dog Wishbone died. I connected with our local shelter, which provided free training for me so I was prepared to visit local nursing homes and hospitals with my own trained pet or take part in the visit with other pets. These loving outreach visits were very much appreciated by the people in these facilities, and their smiles and laughter were priceless. I truly enjoyed my time in this endeavor; it is really true that you get back so much more than you give when you volunteer.

For me, it was exciting to see all the animals entering the facilities. We brought in a whole entourage of dogs, cats, and rabbits to visit the residents. The atmosphere in the room magically changed in seconds. The animals and their humans were specially trained for animal-assisted activities and prepared to interact with the people. Eyes lit up when the smaller animals in baskets were placed on the willing lap of the recipient, who showered the animal with their special love. The larger animals quietly stood by as others would reach for a gentle pet and silently speak special words of love to the animal.

I can attest to moods that changed as the animals and residents interacted. It was amazing to watch facial expressions change and the mood of the room become filled with warmth. I could hear soft purrs and words that spoke of happiness that these beautiful healing animals were present. The room became a healing vessel for these folks during our visit. It was calming as young and old stroked the animals and talked with them. I saw the smiles as the people engaged with the furry visitors. When it was time to leave, they happily asked, "Can you come again?" and we did. The visits validated to me the power of animals to heal and the enormous benefits they provide. In the end, I was greatly rewarded by the sights and signs of this experience. The love between animal and human was on display. I was truly fortunate for the opportunity to be a volunteer for these experiences.

LINKING OBJECTS

Linking objects can be an image or physical object that you feel connects you to your beloved pet. They can remind you of your emotional connection with your pet and help to keep you connected closely to your pet in a way that is different now.

The linking object can provide you with a sense of comfort and create a sense of closeness to them. It can be especially helpful early on after the loss of your pet.

You can attach your pet's name tag to your keychain or something else that you frequently carry with you. It brings some comfort knowing your pet is traveling along with you as you carry and use your keys. Also, with some linking objects, it is the touch that provides the link. A few clippings of fur from your pet or their favorite toy might provide comfort to you. One of my clients dealing with the loss of her pet found that stroking her deceased pet's fur early on brought peace and comfort.

JEWELRY

There are many online companies that offer various types of jewelry specially designed for pet remembrances, such as bracelets, necklaces, and decorative pins. Local jewelers in your area may carry items that can be engraved with your pet's name or other message. Many artists who create jewelry may be found at craft fairs. They may be able to create a one-of-a-kind jewelry item for you to remember your pet.

CREATING WITH YOUR HANDS

You could also try your hand at making something yourself. For me, the act of creating something myself, or with someone else, has more meaning than purchasing something that is mass-produced. Here are a few examples of what you can do with your hands to make a remembrance of your pet.

Pictures

Children can draw pictures of the family pet and share what the pictures mean to them. It's better not to try to interpret their pictures, but rather to have them describe their picture in their own words. Encourage them to hang their picture in a special place. They may find some comfort if it is hanging in their bedroom or in a special place in the house in which the family frequently congregates.

Scrapbook

There are many ways to make up a scrapbook, and the whole family can take part. This project may take some time, so it would be a good idea to set aside specific times when it can be worked on together as a family, acknowledging everyone's schedules.

First, it would be a good idea to decide what this scrapbook will hold. Will you purchase a special scrapbook from the store? Will it be done electronically from a website that specializes in scrapbooking? Also, will it contain just photos or include paintings and drawings? Will it include mementos, such as sympathy cards or notes? Think about your life with your pet. When this book is completed and viewed later, it can bring back memorable times to you and your whole family of the time spent with your pet.

Rock Painting

Small smooth stones or rocks are available for purchase at garden stores and some craft stores as well as online. Create one with your pet's name or a paw print or a special quote. Paint it or decoupage it. If you start painting and designing a rock and decide you don't like it, just paint over it and start anew. Have fun and enjoy the relaxing healing effects it can have on you, with the end result of creating a remembrance of your pet.

Collage

There are endless possibilities in creating a collage, with no artistic talent needed. Pictures and words from magazines can all be incorporated into a collage that speaks to you and your relationship with your pet. You can also incorporate other found items, bits of material, and scraps of wallpaper.

Painting

Ever think of having an artist create a painting of your pet? Pick out one of your favorite photos, and an artist can create a beautiful, one-of-a-kind painting for that special place in your home. Photos are great, but a painting can be dramatic and makes for a special remembrance of your pet. There are many artists who specialize in painting animals.

Clay Sculpture

Try your hand at creating something out of clay that reminds you of your cherished pet. Like the rock painting, if at first you don't feel you succeeded, it's easy to go back and start over.

Sewing Project

You can make a variety of sewing projects in memory of your pet, including bandannas for cats and dogs to be donated to a shelter, a pillow with your pet's name on it, a needlework picture, or a memory quilt. If your pet wore bandannas, you can sew them together into a scarf or a quilt.

If you celebrate Christmas, you can buy or make a stocking for your pet. You can add items to it on a regular basis (maybe every day during Advent) and donate them to a rescue organization or animal shelter in your pet's memory.

Holiday Decorations

If you celebrate Christmas, you can make or buy a special ornament for your tree in memory of your pet. You can make a suitable decoration for other holidays you celebrate.

WEBSITE OR POWERPOINT PRESENTATION

A website can be created in your pet's memory. This can be a great project if someone in the family is really into technology and knows how to set up a website. Pictures and other postings can be compiled in memory of your life with your pet. If you are not interested in a website, as hosting fees and establishing one may be beyond your budget, you can try a PowerPoint presentation. This is something that I created in memory of my dog Wishbone. It contains pictures of him with descriptions of the many happy times shared with him and our family. It's very meaningful, as you can view and enjoy it whenever you wish, and it always brings the treasured times back to life with smiles and good feelings for the viewers.

MEMORIAL VIDEO

If you have videos of your pet, you can either combine them yourself or have a video service combine them into a memorial video of your pet. You can add scenes of people sharing memories about your pet and how important they were in their lives.

Investing time in projects that remember my pets has brought me much peace. My hope is that one or several of these activities can do the same for you. Whatever helps you to remember your pet is what is important here. You are the one who knows what will be helpful and possible for you to do. Think about it, and then make a plan to do something that you feel will give you joy. You can do this! Remember, they have left this world, but not our hearts!

REFLECTIVE WRITING EXPERIENCES

CHAPTER 11:

Remembering and Honoring Your Pet

Consider any of the many ways you can honor your pet from the ideas in this chapter, or come up with your own ideas. These ideas can be a tangible way to continue to cope with your grief and ultimately honor the memory of your pet. When you engage in these activities, the result is something you can see and touch or hold in your hand as a reminder of the bond of love you had with your pet during their life. It will be a reminder of all the wonderful memories that you can always treasure.

Writing Experience # 1—Haiku Poem or Any Other Type of Poem

You might want to try your hand at writing your own haiku. A haiku is a traditional Japanese poem, consisting of three short unrhymed lines of five, seven, and five syllables. The origins of haiku poems can be traced back as far as the ninth century. Haiku often features an image, or a pair of images, meant to depict the essence of a specific moment in time. You can brainstorm some words about your pet or your feelings, and then write haiku poetry. Put the poem in a book or a double-sided frame that also has a picture of your cherished pet. Here is a second example haiku for my dog Wishbone:

Around The Tree Go
Wishy Dog Chasing Running
Squirrel Alert Go!

Writing Experience #2—Gratitude

In a special decorative book, make a list of all the wonderful things you shared with your pet that you are grateful for (such as "Your silly antics always made me laugh and feel good," "You were my stress buster," and "I loved having your companionship in my life").

Writing Experience #3— A Plan for Honoring Your Pet's Memory

Have you decided on what you may do to honor the memory of your pet? Write out a plan on how you will accomplish it. Will you need to buy any supplies, do additional research, or engage the help of others? Come up with a plan on how and when you will do it. A written plan will make it easier to accomplish your project. It can be a welcomed fun activity and above all else a healing experience.

"The greatness of a nation and its moral progress can be judged by the way its animals are treated."

—MAHATMA GANDHI

SECTION IV

Moving Forward

I hope you will reread parts of the compassionate guidance of this book as you continue on your journey of grief. Reading it again will allow you to find new perspectives that you might not have seen during your first reading.

This is a guidebook to accompany you during this loss and future losses that are an inevitable part of life. Losing a cherished pet helps to remind us of how precious life is. We can emerge from the pain and find deeper meaning in our lives. Since each loss is unique, the information that has served you well for this particular grief journey may be different from subsequent losses. I hope your newfound understanding of the human–animal bond helps you understand why this particular loss hurts so much.

Chapter 12

Embracing Change, Recognizing Hope

any of the changes are painfully obvious right now, and additional changes will keep appearing, some soon and others much later. For example, maybe now you have begun to slow down and embrace the moment and understand the importance of taking care of yourself more. Later, you may become more open to trying new things. Consider embracing the changes as they occur; know that you have a special purpose on this earth and that there is always hope.

"For our people, butterflies are a symbol of hope. It's said that if you capture one in your hands and whisper your dreams to it, it will carry them up to the heavens so that the wish can be granted."

—SHERRILYN KENYON

This chapter presents you with new opportunities to consider as you move along in your grief journey. A loss brings many changes to our lives, and as time moves on, you will increasingly adapt to the changes that this loss has brought. Grief eventually transforms into a focus on the wonderful memories created with your pet. A loving relationship with a pet is built over many shared experiences. Staying connected to your pet after their death through remembrances of them can help you cope with their loss and all the accompanying changes brought by this loss. Life will be different without the pet that you have lost. If you someday decide to bring another pet into your life, it will never be a replacement for the cherished pet that died or is otherwise gone.

As you move on from this book, my hope is that you have gained a deeper understanding of the loss you have endured. Remember, it takes time. Your grief will likely continue to ebb and flow. Whether your pet was in your life for a short time or for many years, your life now contains a large void. It is an adjustment and a change. It may even be a wake-up call. We are never really prepared for death, and when it hits us, it hits hard. When you started this journey of grief, did you know that grief is a teacher in our lives? Among the many things our pets have taught us, they have also taught us about our own mortality. You have grown from this loss in many ways. Some you may recognize now, and new growth will likely occur later.

A Changed Routine

As you move around your home and miss the presence of your cherished pet, you might want to consider the possibility of rearranging some of your surroundings. It may be too hard to walk past the area where your pet slept or spent a lot of their time. Perhaps making some minor changes around the house can soften the reality so that you are not always looking for your pet in those places where they used to be. You may find comfort in seeing their special toys, or you may feel it's best to donate some of the items that they used to an animal shelter. Keep in mind that there is no single best answer for this, except to take your time, think it through, and decide what to do when you feel stronger. Your routine has changed; sometimes, the things you did for your pet defined the beginning and ending of your day and many of the times in between. For some of those routines, you can now add an activity of remembering your pet. Maybe their food and water bowls were in the kitchen and you cleaned and refilled them each day. Think about putting a live house plant near that spot, and care for it in your pet's memory. You may want to put a small picture of your pet near the plant. In addition to many physical changes in your routine, you have also lost the special emotional support your cherished pet provided: the calming effect that they had in your life, their gift for soothing you through a difficult time. It has been a trying time, and you are beginning to adjust to the changes resulting from their loss while keeping their memory close to you. Be patient with yourself. It takes time to adjust. It is never easy.

ANOTHER PET?

Maybe you are thinking at this time, "Do I want to bring another pet into my life? When is the right time? Will I feel guilty because I want to acquire another pet so soon? Am I trying to replace the pet I had?" These questions may be swirling around in your mind and in your heart. Sometime in the future you may consider bringing another lucky pet into your home and heart. It might not be now. You will know in your heart; there will come a time when you will feel that this is the right time. You already are prepared, and know that it will be another unique pet with all of its own silly antics and special love for you. It will not be a betrayal of your previous beloved pet, who is physically gone from your life. Whoever becomes your lucky pet, give them your love and care and celebrate the human–animal bond you share.

I recommend that, if you choose to bring another pet into your life, you really reflect and consider your specific situation. You need to discuss it with other family members and determine their thoughts on bringing another pet into the family. Everyone who will be interacting with a new pet needs to feel comfortable with the decision. Some may not be ready or may feel some resentment if a new pet is acquired too soon.

This decision can also involve other family pets, who enjoyed their life with and had a bond with the pet who died. Perhaps a prospective new furry addition to the family can meet the current furry members, to see if they get along. If there are any concerns, it would be good to discuss them with your veterinarian. There is a definite adjustment for them as well, and they will continue to need extra attention as they grieve in their own special way.

It will be important for everyone to feel they have worked sufficiently through their own grief. At that point there will be more confidence that you can look forward to a new relationship with an addition to your family. You will enjoy and learn about this pet whose special qualities will pave the way for you to move into this new relationship. New adventures and memories will form with this new family member.

You may also want to consider a different size or breed of pet, or one that has very different markings from your previous pet. You may inadvertently project negative feelings onto this new family member if he or she reminds you too much of the one you lost.

Alternatively, you may want to try being a foster pet parent for a while and help another pet learn some socialization skills. You would also experience firsthand how it feels to have another pet in the household once again, and learn how family members or other pets interact with a new pet.

If you are considering a puppy, it is important to remember the exuberant puppy behavior that you may not have dealt with for a long time. If you have older pets in the household, you need to consider if they will be tolerant of this younger pet. Of course, a new pet may actually help revitalize the oldster!

You may know other people who have lost a pet and eventually brought another into their family. Ask if you can talk with them about this, and use the information to help guide you in your decision. You may find that it is not a wise choice for you right now. If you decide that bringing another family pet into your home is not a good choice, that will be the right decision for you. You may decide not to adopt another companion animal because of the emotional, physical, or financial demands involved.

There are other options you might want to consider. Review some of the many volunteering opportunities that are detailed in Chapter 11; these would allow you to have a pet in your life but not as a part of your family. So much good can be done by volunteering!

 ## NEW OPPORTUNITIES

Maybe now it would be good to seek out some new interests and reassess some areas of your life. Decide each day what you can do to support your emotional and physical well-being. Stay motivated and be a part of life. Joy will return; be open to it. Engage in stress-reducing activities.

Every week, schedule something specific in your calendar that you do for *yourself*. Go for that long walk in nature if you are able, and notice the beauty of the earth. Learn something new, engage with friends and family, and continue to experience life. Enjoy looking at old photos, and reminisce about the happy times with your pet. Focus on the positive possibilities before you. You have been through a lot.

> *"Hope is being able to see that there is light despite all of the darkness."*
> —DESMOND TUTU

Take your time and be sure you have had sufficient time to deal with all the emotions of your grief.

WHEN WILL I GET THROUGH THIS?

Many clients have asked me, "How long does it take to get over or through this loss? How long will the pain go on?" Everyone deserves as much time as they need to address and work through their emotions. There is no particular schedule for grief. It is a process that takes time. How long that will take is different for everyone, so comparisons about how long somebody else needed will not be helpful. Your actual timeline is related to your particular attachment to your pet and all the other circumstances that make up who you are. These include your pet's age, other pets in the household, your personality, your personal situation at the time of your pet's death, and your cultural and religious beliefs. Stay connected to life, and when you are feeling up to it, engage in something from Chapter 11 to honor your pet's memory.

Be patient with yourself and take the time to express and process all your emotions. Some days it may feel like you are taking baby steps to feeling better in your grief journey. For example, you might notice that you are better able to function at home or in an outside work environment. Maybe you are better able to feel control over the extremes in your emotions. It is important to create time and space in your schedule to just sit, reflect, and have a good cry. Eventually, the focus will be more on the wonderful memories that were created between you and your very special pet. Most important is to continue to work through all of your feelings and not repress them. Your relationship with your pet was built over many shared experiences, and their loss has created a void in your life. Your life has been forever changed because of this loss. You can feel better, move forward, and honor and cherish the memory of your beloved pet. Continue to reach out to others who understand the loss, even though you may also encounter others who do not fully understand. Your grief simply means you loved deeply. Be gentle with yourself.

You Did Your Best

Remember, you did your best, always loving and caring for your pet. You know that your beloved pet will always be present in your heart. You have gained some tools to cope with this loss. You are equipped to help others as well, because you have experienced a loss, and you know the impact that losing a cherished pet has on your life. The loss of a pet can be a catalyst for personal growth. Having experienced this loss gives you firsthand knowledge that can allow you to more fully understand someone else's grief. Hang in there and know you are not alone! We truly are all in this together.

Be patient with your healing journey. Honor the memory of your cherished companion, and always embrace hope. Each pet who has been lucky to be in your life occupies their very own carved-out place in your heart where they will always rest. Your heart is big, and there will always be room for the memories of every pet in your life. Remember that your cherished, unique pet will always live in your heart with all the precious memories you created and shared over the years. These memories can be accessed and continue to bring joy into your life. This is something that I have experienced myself when I speak of my previous pet relationships. You will always enjoy your memories when you talk about your cherished pet. I believe a warm smile will form on your face, and you will experience the joy and gratitude for the life they shared with you.

As always, I wish you well and much peace,

 anne Marie

Appendix A

BOOKS FOR CHILDREN ON GRIEF AND LOSS

Here is a short list of sensitive books and caring stories about pet loss that were written for children but can be just as helpful and comforting to adults. When a book is read to a child, it can spark a question in them that needs to be explored with a loving, caring adult. It can serve as a catalyst for more discussion and understanding of their grief.

All God's Creatures Go to Heaven, Amy Nolfo-Wheeler (Noël Studio, Inc., 1996)

The Fall of Freddie the Leaf: A Story of Life for All Ages, Leo Buscaglia (Slack, 1982)

It Must Hurt a Lot: A Child's Book about Death, Doris Sanford (Multnomah Press, 1986)

Lifetimes: The Beautiful Way to Explain Death to Children, Bryan Mellonie and Robert Ingpen (Bantam Books, 1983)

Tear Soup, Pat Schweibert (Grief Watch, 2005)

The Tenth Good Thing about Barney, Judith Viorst (Macmillan, 1971)

When a Pet Dies, Fred Rogers (Putnam, 1988)

Appendix B

RESOURCES FOR SUPPORT

Phone Numbers

To find a pet loss support group in your area, contact your local veterinarian for recommendations, find them online on your veterinary hospital's website, or search for groups in your area. Here are some examples of support hotlines:

Illinois
Chicago, Illinois, VMA
(630) 325-1600
The helpline is available anytime. Calls will be returned 7:00 p.m. to 9:00 p.m. Long-distance calls will be returned collect.

Maryland and Virginia
The Virginia-Maryland Regional College of Veterinary Medicine Helpline: (540) 231-8038

Massachusetts
Tufts University School of Veterinary Medicine
Pet Loss Support Hotline: (508) 839-7966
Messages left during off-hours will be returned, at no cost to the caller, during the next normal hotline shift. During the academic year, the hotline is available Monday through Thursday, 6:00 p.m. to 9:00 p.m. EST. During the summer, hours vary. Please call for more information.

New Jersey

St. Hubert's Animal Welfare Center

Meg M. Struble

Vice President of Operations

575 Woodland Avenue

Madison, NJ 07940

(973) 377-7094

For the past eight years, St. Hubert's has offered pet loss support group sessions at no cost every Tuesday evening at their facility. Individual sessions are also available for a nominal fee.

New York

Cornell University College of Veterinary Medicine

Pet Loss Support Hotline: (607) 218-7457

The pet loss support hotline is available via Google Voice to facilitate support remotely on Tuesdays, Thursdays, and Saturdays from 6:15 p.m. to 9:15 p.m. EST. Google Voice will prompt you to enter your name before connecting; however, to remain anonymous, you can say "anonymous" or just enter your first name.

Oregon

Dove Lewis Emergency Animal Hospital

Pet Loss Support Services, 24-Hour Message Line: (503) 234-2061

Dove Lewis has provided free pet loss support groups in the Portland, Oregon, area since 1986. Long-distance calls will be returned collect. Emails can be sent to their grief counselor, Director of Pet Loss Support Services Enid Traisman, MSW, at etjournl@teleport.com. Visit their website at www.dovelewis.org.

Tennessee

University of Tennessee College of Veterinary Medicine

Support Line: (865) 755-8839

The support line is available Monday through Friday, 9:00 a.m. to 6:00 p.m.

Web Links

For a list of suggestions for a bucket list for your pet, visit https://bucketlistjourney.net/ideas-for-your-dog-bucket-list/.

I have established the Rochester Center for Pet Grief and Loss (https://www.petlossroc.com/), whose mission is to offer support individually and through groups for people who are experiencing grief because a beloved pet has died, or for anyone with a past loss that they never had the opportunity to fully mourn. One of my goals is to provide education to the community on the importance of understanding and validating pet grief and loss, through individual and group support, presentations, and outreach. If you like, send me an email of how you chose to honor your pet or what you found to be helpful to you in this book. If you give me permission, I will post a limited number of submissions on the "Rochester Center for Pet Grief and Loss" Facebook page. I would love to hear from you.

Appendix C

PLANNING FOR YOUR PET IN THE EVENT OF AN EMERGENCY

We never know when an emergency may occur. It can mean being away from our family pet for a short period of time or a permanent departure from a familiar setting. Having preparations in advance can help ease some of the turmoil that may ensue and help keep our pets safe and part of our lives. Here are some suggestions from the American Society for the Prevention of Cruelty to Animals (ASPCA) disaster preparedness website (ASPCA 2021):

- Obtain a rescue alert sticker for your home, from either this site or a local source. It can alert rescue workers to be aware of pets inside your home.

- Please do not leave your pets behind, as they could become trapped or be exposed to serious hazards. Ask your vet if they have a list of preferred boarding kennels or facilities in case of a disaster.

- Identify hotels or motels outside of your immediate area that accept pets, or ask relatives or friends outside of your immediate area if they would be willing to take in your pet in case of an emergency.

- Consider a temporary caregiver. Carefully consider that this is a person to whom you are entrusting the care of your pet if something should happen to you. Give thought to people who know your pet and have successfully cared for animals in the past. Discuss carefully with this person your expectations so that there are no misunderstandings.

❧ Plan for a worst-case scenario—an evacuation, pandemic, or other disaster—by preparing a kit with essential supplies for your pet. Include a thirty-day supply of your pet's medications, at least a two-week supply of food, and a seven-day supply of water. Choose a friend, neighbor, or loved one who could help if you are unable to care for your pet, and let them know where the kit is stored and whom to contact in case veterinary care is needed. The kit should include up-to-date identification of your pet and recent photographs. Your pet's ID tag should include their name, your name, and your contact information. If you have a pet carrier, also put that information on it. Microchipping is recommended by the ASPCA. Store the emergency kit and leashes near the exit of your home. Rotate consumable supplies, such as food and water, every two months. For a complete list of what to put in this emergency kit, please check out https://www.aspca.org/pet-care/general-pet-care/disaster-preparedness.

Bibliography

ADA National Network. 2017. "Service Animals." ADA National Network, Mid-Atlantic ADA Center. https://adata.org/sites/adata.org/files/files/Service_Animals_final2017.pdf_

Alliance of Therapy Dogs. 2017. "The Modern Use of Animal Assisted Therapy." https://www.therapydogs.com/animal-assisted-therapy/.

American Heart Association. 2013. "Pet Ownership and Cardiovascular Risk: A Scientific Statement from the American Heart Association." *Circulation* vol. 127, no. 23: 2353–2363. https://www.ahajournals.org/doi/reader/10.1161/CIR.0b013e31829201e1.

American Kennel Club. 2020. "What Is Canine Good Citizen?" https://www.akc.org/products-services/training-programs/canine-good-citizen/what-is-canine-good-citizen/.

American Society for the Prevention of Cruelty to Animals (ASPCA). 2021. "Disaster Preparedness." https://www.aspca.org/pet-care/general-pet-care/disaster-preparedness.

American Veterinary Medical Association, Veterinary Economics Division. 2018. *2017–2018 AVMA Pet Ownership & Demographics Sourcebook.* Schaumburg, IL: American Veterinary Medical Association.

Association for Psychological Science. 2016. "Effective Apologies Include Six Elements." https://www.psychologicalscience.org/news/minds-business/effective-apologies-include-six-elements.html.

Barker, S. B., and A. K. Wolen. 2008. "The Benefits of Human–Companion Animal Interaction: A Review." *Journal of Veterinary Medicine Education.*

Beck, Alan. 2014. "The Biology of the Human–Animal Bond." *Animal Frontiers.* West Lafayette, IN: College of Veterinary Medicine, Perdue University.

Beck, Alan and Aaron Katcher. 1996. *Between Pets and People: The Importance of Animal Companionship.* West Lafayette, IN: Perdue University Press.

Brown, Richard, and Patricia Gerbarg. 2012. *The Healing Power of the Breath.* Boulder, CO: Shambhala Publications.

Brulliard, Karin. 2017. "In a First, Alaska Divorce Courts Will Now Treat Pets More Like Children." *Washington Post*. www.washingtonpost.com/news/animalia/wp/2017/01/24/in-a-first-alaska-divorce-courts-will-now-treat-pets-more-like-children/.

Cain, Susan, and Michael Cain. 2020. "Canine Dementia—Signs, Symptoms, Treatments." *Bark: Dog Is My Co-pilot*. https://thebark.com/content/canine-dementia-signs-symptoms-treatments.

Carroll, Linda. 2016. "Our Dogs Really Do Love Us! Praise Is as Big as Treats for Your Pet." *Today*. https://www.today.com/health/out-dogs-really-do-love-us-praise-big-treats-your-t102041.

Casabianca, Sandra Silva. 2021. *Coping with Grief: How the Ball and the Box Analogy May Help*. http://psychcentral.com/blog/coping-with-grief-ball-and-box-analogy.

Castaldo, Nancy F. 2014. *Sniffer Dogs: How Dogs and Their Noses Save the World*. Boston: Houghton Mifflin Harcourt.

CBS News. 2016. "Some Companies Letting Employees Take Off Work after Pet Dies." https://www.cbsnews.com/news/some-companies-letting-employees-take-off-work-after-pet-dies/.

CBS News. 2017. "Dog Saves Injured Michigan Man from Freezing to Death in the Snow." https://www.cbsnews.com/news/dog-keeps-injured-owner-from-freezing-to-death-in-the-snow/.

Coffey, Laura T. 2014. "Good Kitty: These 6 'Hero Cats' Saved the Humans They Loved." https://www.today.com/pets/good-kitty-these-6-hero-cats-saved-humans-they-loved-2d79677090.

Coren, Stanley. 2002. *The Pawprints of History*. New York: Free Press.

Coren, Stanley. 2012. "Canine Empathy: Your Dog Really Does Care If You Are Unhappy." *Psychology Today*. https://www.psychologytoday.com/us/blog/canine-corner/201206/canine-empathy-your-dog-really-does-care-if-you-are-unhappy.

Fine, Aubrey H. 2010. *Handbook on Animal Assisted Therapy, Third Edition*. San Diego: Academic Press.

Fine, Aubrey H. 2015. *Handbook on Animal Assisted Therapy, Fourth Edition*. San Diego: Academic Press.

Fox, Alex. 2020. "Dogs Are Being Trained to Sniff Out COVID-19." Smithsonianmag.com. https://www.smithsonianmag.com/smart-news/dogs-are-being-trained-detect-covid-19-180974796/

Gee, N. R., M. T. Church, and C. L. Altobelli. 2010. "Preschoolers Make Fewer Errors on an Object Categorization Task in the Presence of a Dog." *Anthrozoös.*

Gee, N. R., J. K. Gould, C. C. Swanson, and A. K. Wagner. 2012. "Preschoolers Categorize Animate Objects Better in the Presence of a Dog." *Anthrozoös.*

Gilbertson, Dawn. 2021. "USA TODAY: Southwest Will Ban Emotional Support Animals in March, Joining American, United, Delta." https://www.usatoday.com/story/travel/airline-news/2021/01/25/southwest-airlines-ban-emotional-support-animals-service-animals-march-1/ 4252488001/.

Grimm, David. 2014. *Citizen Canine: Our Evolving Relationship with Cats and Dogs.* New York: PublicAffairs.

Grimm, David. 2015. "How Hurricane Katrina Turned Pets into People." *BuzzFeed News.* https://www.buzzfeednews.com/article/davidhgrimm/how-hurricane-katrina-turned-pets-into-people.

Hare, Brian, Alexandra Rosati, Juliane Kaminski, Juliane Brauer, Joseph Call, and Michael Tomasello. 2010. "The Domestication Hypothesis for Dogs' Skills with Human Communication: A Response to Udell et al. (2008) and Wynne et al. (2008)." *Animal Behaviour* vol. 79: e1–e6. https://doglab.shh.mpg.de/pdf/Hare_et_al_%202010_%20The_domestication_hypothesis_for_dogs_skills.pdf

Harper, C. M., Y. Dong, T. S. Thornhill, et al. 2014. "Can Therapy Dogs Improve Pain and Satisfaction after Total Joint Arthroplasty? A Randomized Controlled Trial." *Clinical Orthopaedics and Related Research.*

Heady, B., M. Grabka, J. Kelley, P. Reddy, and Y. Tseng. 2002. "Pet Ownership Is Good for Your Health and Saves Public Expenditure Too. Australian and German Longitudinal Evidence." *Australian Social Monitor.*

Human Animal Bond Research Institute. 2016. "Survey: Pet Owners and the Human–Animal Bond." https://habri.org/2016-pet-owners-survey.

Intermountain Therapy Animals. 2020. "R.E.A.D Team Steps." https://therapyanimals.org/read-team-steps/.

Jacobo, Julia. 2019. "Prison Animal Programs Are Benefitting Both Inmates and Hard-to-Adopt Dogs in Florida, Experts Say." https://abcnews.go.com/US/prison-animal-programs-benefitting-inmates-hard-adopt-dogs/story?id=60600864.

Johnson, Rebecca A., and Richard L. Meadows. 2010. "Dog-Walking: Motivation for Adherence to a Walking Program." *PubMed.* https://doi.org/10.1177/1054773810373122.

Karaban, Roslyn. 2000. *Complicated Losses, Difficult Deaths: A Practical Guide for Ministering to Grievers*. San Jose: Resource Publications, Inc.

King, Barbara J. 2014. *How Animals Grieve*. Chicago: The University of Chicago Press.

Kübler-Ross, E. 1969. *On Death and Dying*. New York: Macmillan.

Lagoni, Laurel, Carolyn Butler, and Suzanne Hetts. 1994. *The Human–Animal Bond and Grief*. Philadelphia: W. B. Saunders Company.

Lap of Love Veterinary Hospice & In-Home Euthanasia. 2022. https://www.lapoflove.com/.

Lenhard, Emily. 2018. "The Human–Animal Bond throughout Time." East Lansing Michigan: Michigan State University College of Veterinary Medicine. https://cvm.msu.edu/news/perspectives-magazine/perspectives-fall-2018/the-human-animal-bond-throughout-time.

Levinson, Boris M., and Gerald P. Mallon. 1997. *Pet-Oriented Child Psychotherapy, 2nd Edition*. Springfield, Illinois: Charles C. Thomas Publisher, Ltd.

Liu, Herbert. 2014. "The Difference Between Shame and Guilt, and Why It Matters," *Lifehacker*. https://lifehacker.com/what-you-need-to-know-about-shame-and-guilt-1653163759.

Marcus, Dawn A, Cheryl D. Bernstein, Janet M. Constantin, Frank A. Kunkel, Paula Breuer, and Raymond B. Hanlon. 2013. "Impact of Animal-Assisted Therapy for Outpatients with Fibromyalgia," *Pain Med* vol. 14, no. 1 (January): 43–51.

McVean, Ada. 2019. "It's Time to Let the Five Stages of Grief Die." *Office for Science and Society*, McGill University. https://www.mcgill.ca/oss/article/health-history/its-time-let-five-stages-grief-die.

Melina, Remy. 2010. "Is Having a Pet Good for Your Health?" https://www.livescience.com/32746-is-having-a-pet-good-for-your-health-.html.

National Geographic Partners. 2018. *125 True Stories of Amazing Animal Friendships*. Washington DC: National Geographic Partners.

National Public Radio. 2018. "George H. W. Bush's Service Dog Stays by His Casket." https://www.npr.org/2018/12/03/672852640/george-w-w-bushs-service-dog-stays-by-his-casket.

Ng, Christina. 2011. "Loyal Navy SEAL Dog Hawkeye Finds New Home." *ABC News*. https://abcnews.go.com/US/navy-seal-dog-hawkeye-finds-home/story?id=14428040

O'Haire, M. E., S. J. McKenzie, A. M. Beck, and V. Slaughter. 2013. "Social Behaviors Increase in Children with Autism in the Presence of Animals."

Olmert, Meg Daley. 2009. *Made for Each Other: The Biology of the Human Animal Bond*. Massachusetts: De Capo Press.

Parshall, Debra Phillips. 2003. "Research and Reflection: Animal-Assisted Therapy in Mental Health Settings." *Counseling and Values* vol. 48, no. 1: 47. https://go.gale.com/ps/anonymous?id=GALE%7CA110263446&sid=google Scholar&v=2.1&it=r&linkaccs.

Pet Partners, Inc. 2020. "Research Statistics Compiled by Pet Partners, Inc.: Benefits of the Human–Animal Bond." https://www.therapypartners.org/animal-therapy-research.

Prato-Previde, Emanuela, Deborah Custance, Caterina Spiezio, and Francesca Sabatini. 2003. "Is the Dog-Human Relationship an Attachment Bond? An Observational Study Using Ainsworth's Strange Situation." *Behaviour* vol. 140, no. 2: 225–254. https://doi.org/10.1163/ 156853903321671514.

Reamer, David. 2020. "Togo Was the True Hero of the Serum Run; It's About Time He Got His Due." *Anchorage Daily News*. https://www.adn.com/alaska-life/2020/03/02/togo-was-the-true-hero-dog-of-the-serum-run-its-about-time-he-got-his-due./

Sakson, Sharon. 2009. *Paws & Effect*. New York: Spiegel and Grau.

Salotto, Pearl. 2001. *Pet Assisted Therapy: A Loving Intervention and an Emerging Profession: Leading to a Friendlier, Healthier, and More Peaceful World*. Norton, MA: D. J. Publications.

Schonfeld, Alexandra, 2021. "Court Grants Joint Custody of Dog in 'Pioneering Ruling.'" *Newsweek*. https://www.newsweek.com/court-grants-joint-custody-dog-pioneering-ruling-1643267.

Shmerling, Robert H. 2018. "Dogs and Health: A Lower Risk for Heart Disease-Related Death?" Harvard Health Publishing. https://www.health.harvard.edu/blog/dogs-and-health-a-lower-risk-for-heart-disease-related-death-2018061114020.

Sobo, E. J., B. Eng, and N. Kassity-Krich. 2006. "Canine Visitation (Pet) Therapy: Pilot Study Data on Decrease in Child Pain Perception." *Journal of Holistic Nursing*.

Therapydogs.com. 2020. "The Modern Use of Animal Assisted Therapy." Alliance of Therapy Dogs Inc. https://www.therapydogs.com/animal-assisted-therapy/.

Trahan, G. J., P. M. Bracci, and E. A. Holly. 2008. "Domestic and Farm-Animal Exposures and Risk of Non-Hodgkin's Lymphoma in a Population-Based Study in San Francisco Bay Area." *Cancer Epidemiology, Biomarkers & Prevention.*

United States Department of Transportation. 2020. "US Department of Transportation Announces Final Rule on Traveling by Air with Service Animals." https://www.transportation.gov/briefing-room/us-department-transportation-announces-final-rule-traveling-air-service-animals.

University of Exeter. 2015. "Aquariums Deliver Health and Well-Being Benefits: People Who Spend Time Watching Aquariums and Fish Tanks Could See Improvements in Their Physical and Mental Well-Being." ScienceDaily. www.sciencedaily.com/releases/2015/07/ 150729215632.htm.

Van Fleet, R., and T. Faa-Thompson. 2017. *Animal Assisted Play Therapy.* Sarasota, FL: Professional Resource Press.

Weintraub, Pamela. 2019. *The Ultimate Guide to the Animal Mind.* New York: Centennial Media.

WHAM-TV. 2021. "New Legislation Supports Rights of Pets, Vets and Owners in New York State," https://13wham.com/news/local/gov-hochul-signs-animal-welfare-legislative-package.

Worden, J. William. 2009. *Grief Counseling and Grief Therapy: A Handbook for the Mental Health Practitioner, 4th Edition.* New York: Springer Publishing Company, LLC.

Acknowledgments

This book has been a labor of love for me. It has been living in my heart and spirit and eagerly waiting to reach the heartbroken pet guardian. I am truly grateful to share it with others who can be assisted in their journey of grief. No book is ever truly written alone. Therefore, I'd like to recognize and pass praise on to the following people for their support and encouragement in making this book a reality.

My husband, Elmer, who helped with the initial and continued editing, provided technical support, and above all, for his love and constant support. For helping me to keep focused on the task at hand even when my eyes became heavy and I realized that there was still a lot to do. My son, Steven, for all his love, support, encouragement, and expertise throughout my many projects.

Suzanne Bell, the magnificent editor-in-chief, for her editing expertise and most helpful suggestions from the infancy of this book through publication. Thanks also for providing me with much laughter and encouragement through our emails. (Thanks, Steven, for introducing me to Suzanne!). Gretel Hakanson, Johanna Bond LMHC, and Evelyn Duffy for their professional assistance and helpful feedback for this book.

Signe Kastberg, PhD, for kindly writing her warm foreword and sharing her story about her cherished dog, Muffin. All of the professors in the counseling program at St. John Fisher College, for supporting me in the graduate program for mental health counseling, in particular Signe Kastberg, PhD and Rob Rice, PhD.

Rise Van Fleet, PhD, for all the work she continues to do in the field of play therapy with canines and kids of all ages, and for her helpful feedback. Special thanks to Dr. Isabel Wylie, VMD, for her great care in taking care of our special pets and for her support of my work. To all my colleagues, for all the meaningful work they do to assist others in working through important concerns in their lives.

Sr. Mary Jean, SSJ, teacher, mentor, friend, for believing in my dreams and helping me reach them. In memoriam and always in my heart.

A loving reach out of thanks to family members and friends who have encouraged me to write this book and believed in its importance.

A heartfelt thank you to all my clients, who have bravely shared their stories of loss with me, and who continue to inspire me and propel me to continue my work in this field.

To all the beautiful animals in our lives, who provide us with pure and unconditional love, especially family pets Tippy, Sparky, Wishbone, and Jazzy, who have shared in my life and brought me much joy.

About the Author

ANNE MARIE FARAGE SMITH is a lifelong animal lover and an advocate for all animals. She holds a master of science degree in mental health counseling from St. John Fisher University and a master of science degree in education from Nazareth University, and is a Pet Loss Grief Counseling Trained Professional. As an educator and licensed mental health counselor in private practice, she has offered clinical guidance to many individuals and groups experiencing grief and loss. She currently resides in Rochester, NY, where she enjoys spending time with her family, visiting local parks with her dog, Jazzy, traveling, and pursuing creative activities.

SELECTED TITLES FROM SHE WRITES PRESS

She Writes Press is an independent publishing company
founded to serve women writers everywhere.
Visit us at www.shewritespress.com.

Drinking From the Trough: A Veterinarian's Memoir by Mary Carlson, DVM.
978-1-63152-431-8. The story of a suburban Chicago girl who never
expected to move "out West" and become a veterinarian, let alone owner
and caretaker of cats (many), dogs (two), and horses (some with manners,
some without) in Colorado, but did—and, along the way, discovered the
challenges, tragedies, and triumphs of lives, both human and animal,
well lived.

*Dog as My Doctor, Cat as My Nurse: An Animal Lover's Guide to a Healthy, Happy
& Extraordinary Life* by Carlyn Montes De Oca. $16.95, 978-1-63152-186-
7. A groundbreaking look at how dogs and cats affect, enhance, and
remedy human well-being.

Not a Perfect Fit: Stories from Jane's World by Jane A. Schmidt. $16.95, 978-1-
63152-206-2. Jane Schmidt documents her challenges living off grid,
moving from the city to the country, living with a variety of animals as
her only companions, dating, family trips, outdoor adventures, and
midlife in essays full of honesty and humor.

Feeling Fate: A Memoir of Love, Intuition, and Spirit by Joni Sensel. $16.95,
978-1-64742-339-1. A grief memoir with a paranormal twist, *Feeling Fate*
recounts a fairy tale romance marked by a dark intuition of loss. When
the premonition comes true, Joni—a woman torn between faith and
skepticism—ultimately finds healing from and meaning in her grief
through imagination and insights of the heart.

Four Funerals and a Wedding: Resilience in a Time of Grief by Jill Smolowe.
$16.95, 978-1-93831-472-8. When journalist Jill Smolowe lost four fami-
ly members in less than two years, she turned to modern bereavement
research for answers—and made some surprising discoveries.

Where Have I Been All My Life? A Journey Toward Love and Wholeness by
Cheryl Rice. $16.95, 978-1-63152-917-7. Rice's universally relatable
story of how her mother's sudden death launched her on a journey into
the deepest parts of grief—and, ultimately, toward love and wholeness.